THE REAL TUDORS

THE REAL TUDORS

KINGS AND QUEENS REDISCOVERED

CHARLOTTE BOLLAND
AND TARNYA COOPER

NATIONAL PORTRAIT GALLERY, LONDON

Published in Great Britain by National Portrait Gallery Publications,
St Martin's Place, London WC2H 0HE

Published to accompany the display
The Real Tudors: Kings and Queens Rediscovered
12 September 2014–1 March 2015

This display has been made possible by the provision
of insurance through the Government Indemnity Scheme.
The National Portrait Gallery, London, would like to thank
HM Government for providing Government Indemnity
and the Department for Culture, Media and Sport and
Arts Council England for arranging the indemnity.

Sold to support the National Portrait Gallery, London.
For a complete catalogue of current publications, please
write to the National Portrait Gallery at the address above,
or visit our website at www.npg.org.uk/publications

ISBN 978 1 85514 492 7

A catalogue record for this book is available from the British Library.

10 9 8 7 6 5 4 3 2 1

Printed in Bosnia-Herzegovina

p.2 Elizabeth I, by an unknown Continental artist, *c.*1575
(detail of fig. 90)

Managing Editor Christopher Tinker
Senior Editor Sarah Ruddick
Project Editor Rachel Giles
Production Ruth Müller-Wirth, Geoff Barlow
Design Smith & Gilmour

MIX
Paper from
responsible sources
FSC® C110418

CONTENTS

FOREWORD

The collective image of the English monarchs of the Tudor period is dominated by the famous portrait of Henry VIII, created by Hans Holbein, with a hulk-like, four-square figure, hands on hips and chest thrust forward. Henry was in many senses larger than life, and the drama of his split with the Church of Rome, complex diplomatic relations across Europe and sequence of marital partnerships have informed countless works of fiction as well as colouring the ways in which a portrait might fulfill certain expectations. Equally resonant is the Ditchley portrait of Elizabeth I painted by Marcus Gheeraerts the Younger, which positions her with tremendous symbolic and narrative power, standing, literally, on her country.

When examining these and the portraits of the others who reigned under the Tudor badge – Henry VII, Edward VI, Lady Jane Grey and Mary I – we should perhaps not expect to find personality in the modern sense. These portraits were produced for a purpose: the subjects to be admired rather than understood, either in public locations or, if a miniature, locket or ring, by the owner of the image in private. Artists in their workshops knew that their work was to enhance public reputation.

Making Art in Tudor Britain is the important research project that has led to this special display. Over seven years, nearly all the Gallery's Tudor portraits have been re-examined using contemporary scientific techniques. Along with the examination of key comparative images, this has allowed us to understand so much more of how they were made, copied and distributed.

I am very grateful to Tarnya Cooper and Charlotte Bolland for their excellent overall leadership of the *Real Tudors* project, Sarah Ruddick for editorial work, and Smith & Gilmour for designing this book. My thanks also go to Michael Barrett, Pim Baxter, Nick Budden, Natalia Calvocoressi, Rob Carr-Archer, James Cunningham-Graham, Jo Down, Neil Evans, Ian Gardner, Penny Hughes, John Leslie, Justine McLiskey, Ruth Müller-Wirth, Nicola Saunders, Jude Simmons, Fiona Smith, Liz Smith, Christopher Tinker, Sarah Tinsley, Helen Whiteoak and many other colleagues at the National Portrait Gallery for all their hard work in translating an excellent research project into a fascinating display.

Considerable thanks go to those who have generously lent to the display. Thanks also to the trusts, foundations and individuals who have supported *Making Art in Tudor Britain*, without whom the display and this book would not have been possible.

Sandy Nairne
DIRECTOR, NATIONAL PORTRAIT GALLERY

ACKNOWLEDGEMENTS

This important research would not have been possible without generous support from several major donors and funding bodies, and we are particularly grateful to the British Academy, Esmée Fairbairn Foundation, the Leverhulme Trust, the Mercers' Company and an anonymous donor. We are also very grateful to Bank of America Merrill Lynch, the John S. Cohen Foundation, the Idlewild Trust, the Leche Trust, PF Charitable Trust, the Märit and Hans Rausing Charitable Foundation, and the Arts and Humanities Research Council, who have provided dedicated support for specific elements of this research project.

The *Making Art in Tudor Britain* team:
Dr Tarnya Cooper – Principal Investigator (Chief Curator and Curator of Sixteenth-Century Collections)
Sophie Plender MBE (Senior Research Conservator)
Dr Charlotte Bolland (*Making Art in Tudor Britain* Project Curator)
Sally Marriott (Assistant Research Conservator)
Polly Saltmarsh (Assistant Research Conservator)
Dr Edward Town (Leverhulme Research Assistant)
Catherine Daunt (Assistant Curator and PhD candidate)
Caroline Rae (PhD candidate)
Helen Dowding (Assistant Research Conservator)

This collaborative research has been ably supported through the the work of our academic partners, Professor Maurice Howard at the University of Sussex and Professor Aviva Burnstock at the Courtauld Institute of Art. We are also particularly grateful to Ian Tyers, who undertook the dendrochronlogical analysis, to Kate Stonor and Clare Richardson (Tager Stonor Richardson), who undertook the infared reflectography, and to Libby Sheldon (formerly University College London), who was responsible for the identification of pigments through paint sampling and analysis. We are also very grateful to Rachel Billinge (National Gallery) for her help in the interpretation of infrared reflectograms.

The project was supported by a dedicated team of advisors to whom we are extremely grateful: Rachel Billinge (National Gallery), Klaas Jan van den Berg (Netherlands Institute of Cultural Heritage), Susan Foister (National Gallery), Catharine MacLeod (National Portrait Gallery) and Robert Tittler (Concordia and Carleton Universities).

We are also grateful for help and advice from many colleagues in other institutions including: Annie Ablett (freelance conservator), Xanthe Brooke (Walker Art Gallery), Lorne Campbell (National Gallery), Nicola Clark (Royal Holloway), Rupert Featherstone (Hamilton Kerr Institute), Karen Hearn (University College London), Nicole Ryder (freelance conservator), Jennifer Scott (Royal Collection), Rachel Scott (Tate), Christina Sitwell (National Trust), Marika Spring (National Gallery), David Taylor (National Trust) and Lucy Whitaker (Royal Collection).

INTRODUCTION

The period in which the Tudor dynasty was in power – between 1485 and 1603 – has become one of the best-known and widely studied in British history. The dynasty was the first to establish a stable monarchy after the Wars of the Roses, and the key events of the reigns of the Tudor monarchs – Henry VII, his son Henry VIII and his grandchildren Edward VI, Mary I and Elizabeth I – stand out as some of the most dynamic and influential in the panorama of Britain's past. This period saw the first female monarch, the transition from the traditional Roman Catholic religion to the Protestant faith and the birth of the Church of England. It was the beginning of a period of maritime exploration that witnessed the creation of a fledgling overseas empire in North America and the emergence of an outstanding literary culture, both factors that have served to foreground the widespread use of the English language in later centuries. However, it is the infamous personal stories of the individual monarchs and their courts, particularly the long reigns of Henry VIII and Elizabeth I, that have intrigued us for centuries. Henry's remarkable six marriages, tyrannical determination and willingness to rid himself of those who opposed him, and Elizabeth's virginity and survival in the face of adversity, have needed little embellishment to inspire dramatic re-telling in literature, theatre, opera and film. This book brings together new information about the Tudor monarchs as they were seen in their own time, through painted portraiture. These portraits allow us the vivid experience of meeting the 'real' Tudors, face to face.

PORTRAITS OF THE TUDOR MONARCHS

The Tudors came to prominence at a time when painted portraiture in oil was beginning to flourish across Europe. Monarchs, princes, courtiers, cardinals and bishops, as well as wealthy merchants, began to seek out the best painters to capture their likeness and record their appearance for their family and friends, and for posterity. By the time Henry VIII was employing the talented German artist Hans Holbein the Younger in England, his royal counterparts in Europe had already been active in commissioning distinctive portraits that could serve as royal exemplars. For example, the Holy Roman Emperor Maximilian I had sat for the exceptionally talented German artist Albrecht Dürer in 1519, and François I of France had been painted by the skilled French painter Jean Clouet in the 1530s.

The ability to replicate portrait compositions meant that once a suitable image was created, it could be copied and adapted for wider dissemination without the need for further sittings from the life. This became a particular feature of Tudor portraiture, and many portraits of both Henry VIII and Elizabeth I were painted from pre-established patterns in order to meet a lively demand for their image. From the end of the 1400s until the beginning of the 1600s, portraiture evolved from a simple head and shoulder image – often with an arched top reminiscent of the settings for religious imagery – to more realistic, larger-scale images, often showing the whole person standing in elaborate clothes in richly decorated settings. These grand, full-length formats set a model for royal portraiture that lasted into the twentieth century. Given the distance of over five hundred years, it is probable that many important paintings of the Tudor monarchs have been lost, and unfortunately the survival rate, while extremely difficult to assess, is likely to be less than a third of what was originally painted.

NEW DISCOVERIES AND RECENT RESEARCH

This book is the result of research at the National Portrait Gallery undertaken as part of the *Making Art in Tudor Britain* project. The use of scientific analysis has led to new discoveries and insights into the dating, technique and production of Tudor portraits, and this has allowed us to ask fundamental questions about how, when and why portraits were made. Some of these new findings on the best-known and most important portraits of the Tudor monarchs can be found in this book, and provide fascinating new visual evidence. The scope of the research, which covers a long historical period, has also allowed us to learn more about the practices of painters' workshops, changes in artistic

techniques and the influence of foreign artists in England. Further information on the findings from the *Making Art in Tudor Britain* project – including new research on over 100 Tudor and Jacobean portraits – is available online at www.npg.org.uk/ research/programmes/making-art-in-tudor-britain.php

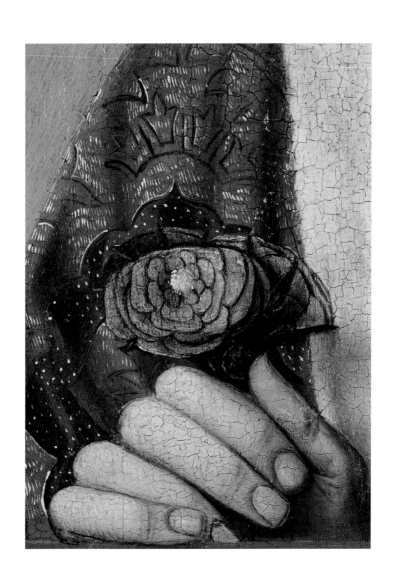

HENRY VII
(1457–1509)

✦

'. . . the Crowne which it pleased
God to geve us . . .

HENRY VII TIMELINE
(REIGNED 1485–1509)

Elizabeth of York

1457
28 January Henry Tudor is born at Pembroke Castle.

Pembroke Castle

1485
7 August Henry Tudor lands at Milford Haven with English, French and Scottish troops.
22 August Battle of Bosworth between the forces of Richard III and Henry Tudor, resulting in Richard's death and Henry's proclamation as king.
30 October Henry Tudor is crowned as Henry VII.

1486
18 January Henry marries Elizabeth of York.
19 September Prince Arthur is born.

1487
24 May Lambert Simnel, an imposter posing as Edward, Earl of Warwick, is crowned in Dublin as 'King Edward VI'.

1470
Henry VI returns to the throne after being deposed in 1461.

Henry VI

1471
Yorkist king Edward IV wins back the throne, and Henry Tudor subsequently flees to France.

Edward IV

1483
Richard, Duke of Gloucester, seizes the throne and is crowned Richard III after the death of Edward IV and the presumed deaths of the King's two sons in the Tower of London.
Henry Tudor's mother, Lady Margaret Beaufort, negotiates Henry's marriage to Edward IV's daughter Elizabeth of York with Edward's widow, Elizabeth Woodville.

Richard III

Margaret Beaufort

1489
28 November Princess Margaret, known as Margaret Tudor, is born.

1491
Perkin Warbeck emerges as a pretender to the English throne.
28 June Prince Henry is born (later Henry VIII).

1499
19 May Proxy marriage of Prince Arthur to Katherine of Aragon.
August Plot attempting to free Perkin Warbeck and Edward Plantagenet, Earl of Warwick, and place one of them on the throne (both are subsequently executed).

Katherine of Aragon

Prince Arthur

1502
2 April Prince Arthur dies suddenly at Ludlow; Katherine of Aragon remains in England.

1494
31 October Prince Henry is made Duke of York in order to counter the threat from Warbeck's claim.

1501
August Edmund de la Pole, Earl of Suffolk, claimant to the English throne, flees England and assumes the Yorkist title of White Rose.
14 November Prince Arthur's marriage to Katherine of Aragon is solemnised at St Paul's Cathedral.

1509
21 April Henry dies at Richmond Palace; he is later buried at Westminster Abbey.

1503
Work begins on the Lady Chapel at Westminster Abbey.
11 February Elizabeth of York dies.
8 August Margaret Tudor marries the Scottish king James IV in Edinburgh.

1497
17 June Cornish rebels are defeated at Blackheath.
23 December Fire destroys the palace at Sheen; Henry subsequently builds Richmond Palace in its place.

Lady Chapel, Westminster Abbey

HENRY'S CLAIM TO THE THRONE

Henry Tudor was the son of Henry VI's half-brother Edmund, 1st Earl of Richmond, and his wife, Margaret Beaufort, great-great-granddaughter of Edward III. As a result, the death of Edward IV in 1483, and the presumed deaths of his young sons in the Tower of London, gave Henry a credible claim to the English throne. After gathering troops in France and Wales he engaged with the much larger forces of Richard III near Market Bosworth on 22 August 1485. Richard was struck down, and Henry was crowned on the battlefield.

Henry's seizure of the English throne made it imperative that he project the image of legitimate kingship. As the French commentator Philippe de Commines astutely noted, Henry had been 'an enemy without power, without money, without right … and without any reputation but what his person and deportment contracted'.[1] He therefore spent lavishly on the maintenance of princely magnificence at court in order to show his wealth and power, with extensive building projects at Richmond Palace, Westminster Abbey and the Savoy Hospital. Of crucial importance was the deployment of his heraldic badges, in particular the Beaufort portcullis and the Lancastrian red rose, which asserted his claim to the throne through his mother's blood and demonstrated his Lancastrian heritage.

Henry's marriage to Edward IV's daughter, Elizabeth of York, and the birth of their son Arthur in September 1486 brought the promise of dynastic stability, and further children followed (fig. 1). However, the years spent moving between Wales, Brittany and France had clearly taken their toll; in 1498 the Spanish diplomat Don Pedro de Ayala reported that 'the King looks old for his years, but young for the sorrowful life he has led'.[2] The most detailed account of Henry's appearance can be found in the history of England that he commissioned from the Italian cleric Polydore Vergil; he was:

> slender but well built and strong; his height above the average. His appearance was remarkably attractive and his face was cheerful, especially when speaking; his eyes were small and blue, his teeth few, poor and blackish; his hair was thin and white; his complexion sallow. His spirit was distinguished, wise and prudent; his mind was brave and resolute and never, even at moments of the greatest danger, deserted him.[3]

Prince Arthur's sudden death in 1502 left the King and Queen distraught, and only one year later Henry became a widower when Elizabeth died shortly after the birth of another daughter, Katherine, who survived for only a few days. The subsequent years of Henry's reign were marked by his declining health and the growing impression that greed lay at the heart of his hold on power. He was described as keeping 'many persons in his danger at his pleasure' through fines, bonds and debts, which created a web of obligation to his rule.[4] This not only filled the Crown's coffers and made Henry's wealth legendary across Europe but also shaped his reputation

in the years immediately following his death. Thus, whilst Henry's reign is now viewed as having brought a degree of order and stability to a chaotic realm, at the time Polydore Vergil was forced to conclude that 'all these virtues were obscured latterly only by avarice … [which] may be considered the worst vice, since it is harmful to everyone, and distorts those qualities of trustfulness, justice and integrity by which the state must be governed'.[5]

Fig. 1 *The Family of Henry VII with St George and the Dragon*, by an unknown Flemish artist, c.1503–9 (The Royal Collection)

Fig. 2 (*above*) Henry VII, by an unknown English artist, early sixteenth century (The Society of Antiquaries)

Fig. 3 (*opposite*) Elizabeth of York, by an unknown English artist, early sixteenth century (The Royal Collection)

THE UNION OF LANCASTER AND YORK

Henry vowed to make Elizabeth of York his wife while in exile in Brittany, as the marriage offered a means of healing the dynastic dispute between the houses of Lancaster and York. However, he ensured that the union was not seen to underpin his claim to the throne by delaying their marriage until after his coronation in October 1485. Although numerous Yorkist plots emerged throughout Henry's reign, with various pretenders to the throne, including Lambert Simnel, Perkin Warbeck and Edmund de la Pole, the image of united red and white roses remained prominent in the pageantry and court poetry of the reign. The alliance also reflected a political reality, with both Lancastrians and Yorkists holding important positions at the court of the new king.

This imagery is incorporated into the most frequently replicated likeness of Henry, in which he is depicted in lavish cloth-of-gold and crimson velvet, holding a red rose. One of the earliest versions of this portrait survives in the Society of Antiquaries, London. This painting retains its original engaged frame, which would have been built around the wooden panel support before painting; it is decorated with the Tudor colours of green and white (fig. 2).

The pose and composition of this image are very similar to the only surviving portrait type of Elizabeth, in which she holds the white rose of York, and this suggests that the two likenesses were intended as companion portraits. The earliest surviving version of Elizabeth's portrait, which may have been painted during her lifetime, is in the Royal Collection (fig. 3), and this may be the painting that hung next to an image of Henry at Westminster Palace during Henry VIII's reign. Portraits of Henry and Elizabeth played an important role in establishing the visual identity of the new dynasty and were sent to James IV in Scotland and to Ferdinand of Aragon and Isabella of Castile in Spain as part of the negotiations for dynastic marriage alliances between their children. These likenesses continued to be replicated long after both the sitters had died.

Fig. 4 (*above*) Henry VII, by an unknown Netherlandish
artist, 1505 (National Portrait Gallery, London)

Fig. 5 (*opposite*) Margaret of Austria, attributed to
Pieter van Coninxloo, c.1500 (The Royal Collection)

A MARRIAGE PORTRAIT

In the years following Elizabeth's death in 1503, Henry considered marrying again in order to form an alliance with another European power. This resulted in the creation of perhaps the most skilfully executed surviving portrait of Henry, which captured his deep-set eyes, high cheekbones and thin lips in 1505 (fig. 4). Most unusually, the inscription records the details of the commission; it states that the portrait was painted at the order of Hermann Rinck, the envoy of the King of the Romans, Maximilian I. Henry is depicted wearing a cap and doublet in his habitual black, regally cloaked in a gown of crimson cloth-of-gold trimmed with ermine. In acknowledgement of the Habsburg audience for the portrait he wears the chain of the Order of the Golden Fleece, to which he had been elected in 1491, rather than the collar of the English chivalric order of the Garter.

The portrait was sent to Maximilian's daughter, the widowed Margaret of Austria, dowager Duchess of Savoy, and an inventory taken at her palace at Malines in 1516 reveals that it was displayed with a red cover painted with vermilion.[6] In exchange, Hermann Rinck brought two portraits of Margaret with him to England for Henry to inspect, one on panel and one on canvas. A third painting may have been sent by Margaret's brother, Philip the Handsome, Duke of Burgundy, from the studio of Pieter van Coninxloo. This was probably a version of an existing portrait rather than a specific commission, and might be the portrait that survives in the Royal Collection (fig. 5).[7] The portraits appear to have been received coolly in England; Katherine of Aragon was of the opinion that another artist would have made a better image.[8] Margaret's desire to remain a widow, which ultimately ensured that the proposal was unsuccessful, probably meant that she was reluctant to sit for a new portrait to support the marriage negotiations.

Neither the inscription, nor the documentation surrounding the marriage negotiations, record the name of the artist who painted Henry's portrait. The paint-handling technique suggests that he was Netherlandish, and he may have been brought to England specifically to undertake the commission. The portrait is thinly painted with fine brushstrokes and careful layering of opaque pigment and glazes. It is possible that, as with the portrait of Margaret that came to England, the painting was one of several versions produced using a pattern based on a drawing taken from the life. However, small changes to the composition, such as adjustments to the fingers and sleeves, indicate that the painting developed as the artist worked. Furthermore, the fact that there are no other surviving versions or copies of the portrait suggests that it was unknown in England as a likeness following the painting's transport to the Low Countries, and was therefore likely to have been a unique image.

Henry also considered a possible marriage to Katherine of Aragon's recently widowed older sister, Joanna of Castile. He let it be known that he would like to have her portrait, but it was noted that neither the young Queen nor her mother should know for whom the portrait was destined, for 'if she proved to be ugly and not handsome the King of England would not have her for all the treasures in the world; nor would he dare to take her, as the English think so much about personal appearance'.[9]

MEMORIAL

Following years of ill health, Henry VII died at Richmond Palace on 21 April 1509. One final likeness was produced for his funeral procession; an effigy that was carried in a traditional rite of monarchy that established the unbroken passage of power from one generation to the next. The effigy was life-size, constructed from a wooden core padded with hay and covered with canvas, with the final modelling for the figure undertaken in plaster. The figure was completed by the addition of a wig and was then dressed in rich robes and laid on golden cushions; the recorded cost was £6 12s 8d, although this could have been the charge for the clothing alone.[10]

The image that was produced can be considered as more than a symbolic representation of the King. It was made by a talented Florentine artist working in England, Pietro Torrigiano, and its detailed characterisation captures Henry's likeness, not in life, but immediately after death (fig. 6). It is evident that the artist used a plaster death mask to make the effigy; the outer edge of the original mask can be seen running along the hairline down the sides of the face to the jaw. The eyes were then 'opened' by carving into the closed lids. The use of plaster, which marked a technical departure for the production of effigies in England, allowed for much more detailed characterisation and subtle modelling of

Fig. 6 Funeral effigy of Henry VII, attributed to Pietro Torrigiano, 1509 (Westminster Abbey)

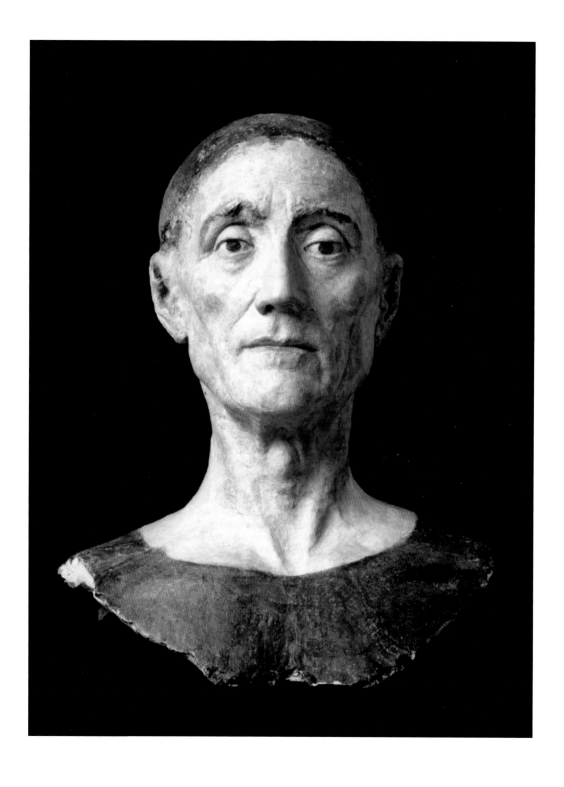

colour and form. By comparison Elizabeth of York's effigy, which was carved from wood by the Swabian sculptor Lawrence Emler in 1503, presents a much less individualistic depiction of the Queen (fig. 7).

A terracotta bust of Henry survives with markedly similar proportions to the effigy head, and it is clear that the artist again used the death mask as the foundation for the portrait (fig. 8). However, this image has been animated and fleshed out, using the artist's skill to bring the image of the dead King to life. By contrast, when the Florentine was commissioned to make the King's tomb, which incorporated recumbent effigies of Henry and Elizabeth, he refined the image. This produced an appropriately timeless portrait, with none of the lifelike texture that could be rendered in plaster and terracotta, but instead the eternal magnificence of gilt bronze (fig. 9).

Fig. 7 (*opposite, above*) Funeral effigy of Elizabeth of York, by Lawrence Emler, 1503 (Westminster Abbey)

Fig. 8 (*opposite, below*) Henry VII by Pietro Torrigiano, 1509–11 (Victoria and Albert Museum)

Fig. 9 (*above*) Detail of Henry VII and Elizabeth of York's tomb, by Pietro Torrigiano, 1512–17 (Lady Chapel, Westminster Abbey)

Cor Regis inscrutabile

Iohn Payne sculpsit.

AFTERLIVES

Henry VII's posthumous reputation was greatly shaped by Sir Francis Bacon's *Historie of the raigne of King Henry the Seventh*, which was first published in 1622. In the dedication of this work to the young Stuart prince Charles (later Charles I), Bacon drew an analogy with the process of portraiture, stating of the King that:

> I have not flattered him, but tooke him to life as well as I could, sitting so farre of, and having no better light.[11]

The book's frontispiece was illustrated with a print by the English engraver John Payne, which depicted Henry holding the sceptre and orb of state, emblazoned with the maxim from Proverbs 25: 3, 'Cor Regis inscrutabile' (The King's heart is inscrutable) (fig. 10).

Henry had attempted to shape his own reputation during the final years of his reign, not only through commissioning Polydore Vergil's history of England but also in visual terms. His will included an instruction that his executors should:

> cause to be made an Ymage of a King, representing our owen persone, the same Ymage to be of tymber, covered and wrought accordingly with plate of fine gold, in maner of an armed man … with a swerd and spurres accordingly … and holding betwixt his hands the Crowne which it pleased God to geve us, with the victorie of our Ennemye at our furst felde.[12]

Fig. 10 Henry VII, by John Payne, 1622 (National Portrait Gallery, London)

The life-size image was to kneel on the shrine of St Edward the Confessor in Westminster Abbey, where it would be visible to all. However, this impressive monument to his triumph as a young man on the field at Bosworth was never made.

Artists who wished to depict Henry after his death were forced to draw on those likenesses that survived. The first to face this challenge was Hans Holbein the Younger, who included portraits of Henry VII and Elizabeth of York in the great dynastic mural executed for Henry VIII at Whitehall Palace, which was completed in 1537. Only the preparatory drawing for this work (known as a cartoon) survives, but there is also a painted copy of the whole composition that was made by Remigius van Leemput at the request of Charles II in 1667. It is notable that in the cartoon Henry VII is depicted in a long, dark velvet robe, with a golden doublet, as he is shown in the Society of Antiquaries portrait (figs 2 and 11), whereas in the completed painting he was evidently depicted in a lavish robe made entirely from cloth-of-gold (fig. 12). This change may provide insight into the difference between Henry VII's self presentation and that of his son: the old king was known for favouring sombre, if expensive, black cloth, while Henry VIII – who commissioned the mural years after his father's death – embraced the flamboyant possibilities of lavish textiles woven with metal threads. Even more remarkable are the differences between Henry VII's portrait in the cartoon and that in the painted copy. For the earlier image Holbein may have drawn on Torrigiano's

sculpted portraits of the King, but the likeness in the final painting is much closer to that seen in the Society of Antiquaries portrait. This change may reflect Holbein's own decisions when completing the mural, as it could have become apparent that for the likeness to be instantly recognisable it needed to derive from a painted image that was familiar from its many versions. However, it could also reflect the effects of repairs made to the mural in the century between its execution and the production of van Leemput's copy, when artists may have used for reference the image of Henry VII that survived in paintings in the Royal Collection.

This pattern for Henry's likeness was certainly popular in the late sixteenth and early seventeenth century, when numerous portrait sets depicting English monarchs were commissioned. These could evidently be made relatively swiftly, with workshops producing batches of paintings. For example, wood from the same trees can often be identified in the boards of different

Fig. 11 (*opposite*) Cartoon for the *Whitehall Mural*, showing Henry VIII and Henry VII, by Hans Holbein the Younger, 1536–7 (National Portrait Gallery, London)

Fig. 12 (*left*) Detail from *Henry VII, Elizabeth of York, Henry VIII and Jane Seymour*, by Remigius van Leemput, 1667 (The Royal Collection)

paintings within sets, suggesting that the panel supports were made at the same time. These paintings often vary in quality, but the portraits of the Tudor monarchs are often the most skilfully executed images in the sets, possibly because the artists were able to work from stronger source images (fig. 13). It is notable that by this point the features and clothing had often been reduced to a simplistic diagram (fig. 14) – which could nonetheless create the recognisable image of a king.

Fig. 13 (*above left*) Henry VII, by an unknown artist, late sixteenth century (National Portrait Gallery, London)

Fig. 14 (*left*) Digital infrared reflectogram detail showing the simple underdrawing in the face.

SELECT BIBLIOGRAPHY

S. Anglo, *Images of Tudor Kingship* (Seaby, London, 1992)

J.A. Franklin, B. Nurse and P. Tudor-Craig, *Catalogue of Paintings in the Collection of the Society of Antiquaries of London* (Harvey Miller Publishers, Brepols Publishers for the Society of Antiquaries of London, London, 2014)

C. Galvin and P. Lindley, 'Pietro Torrigiano's Portrait Bust of King Henry VII', *The Burlington Magazine*, 130, no.1029, 1988, pp.892–902

S. Gunn, 'Henry VII (1457–1509)', *Oxford Dictionary of National Biography* (Oxford University Press, Oxford, 2004), XXVI, pp.510–22

F. Hepburn, 'The 1505 portrait of Henry VII', *Antiquaries Journal,* 88, 2008, pp.222–57

J. Scott, 'Painting from life? Comments on the Date and Function of the Early Portraits of *Elizabeth Woodville* and *Elizabeth of York* in the Royal Collection', *The Yorkist Age: Proceedings of the 2011 Harlaxton Symposium,* H. Kleineke and C. Steer (eds), Harlaxton Medieval Studies, XXIII (Shaun Tyas, Donington, 2013), pp.18–26

R. Strong, 'Henry VII' in *Tudor & Jacobean Portraits,* National Portrait Gallery, 2 vols (HMSO, London, 1969), I, pp.149–52

NOTES

1 *The Memoirs of Philip de Comines*, 2 vols (G. & W.B. Whittaker, London, 1823), II, p.81

2 G.A. Bergenroth et al. (eds), *Calendar of Letters, Despatches, and State Papers Relating to the Negotiations Between England and Spain Preserved in the Archives at Simancas and Elsewhere* (*CSPS*), 13 vols (London, 1862–1954), I, no.210, p.178

3 D. Hay (trans. and ed.), 'The Anglica Historia of Polydore Vergil', *Camden Society*, 3rd series, 74 (1950), p.145

4 C.J. Harrison, 'The Petition of Edmund Dudley', *The English Historical Review*, 87, no.342, 1972, p.86

5 Hay, op. cit., p.147

6 F. Checa Cremades (ed.), *Los inventarios de Carlos V y la familia imperial*, 3 vols (Fernando Villaverde Ediciones, Madrid, 2010), III, p.2392

7 L. Campbell, *The Early Flemish Pictures in the Collection of Her Majesty the Queen* (Cambridge University Press, 1985), pp.34–5

8 *CSPS*, op. cit., I, no.439, p.370. On seeing the paintings in England, Katherine of Aragon was of the opinion that they were not well executed and that another artist, 'Michel', would have made better images.

9 Ibid., no.419, p.344

10 W.H. St John Hope, 'On the Funeral Effigies of the Kings and Queens of England, with Special Reference to Those in the Abbey Church of Westminster', *Archaeologia*, 60, 1906, pt 2, pp.517–65

11 F. Bacon, *Historie of the raigne of King Henry the Seventh* (W. Stansby for Matthew Lownes and William Barret, London, 1622)

12 T. Astle (ed.), *The Will of King Henry VII* (Printed for the editor, London, 1775), pp.35–6

HENRY VII REVEALED

Henry VII
Unknown Netherlandish artist, 1505
Oil on panel, 425×305mm
NPG 416

Images captured using infrared reflectography reveal the strong underdrawing in the face, which appears to have been based on a pattern and then strengthened. By contrast, the drawing in the fingers is much sketchier, and it is evident that the artist worked out the position of the hands while making the portrait, rather than copying from a pattern.

X-radiography reveals pale areas near the hands, which
suggest that the artist originally intended to depict the
King with wide cuffs to his robe. It also shows old nails
around the edge that may relate to an early cover for
the painting when it was in the collection of Margaret
of Austria, Duchess of Savoy.

Photography in ultraviolet light shows that the paint surface is very damaged. The extent of the abrasion may account for the lack of refinement in areas such as the eyes, which appear very simply executed in comparison to the fine detail of the golden chain.

The painting and its integral frame were carved from
a single oak panel, as can be seen from the reverse.
Dendrochronology (tree-ring dating) shows that the
tree used to make the board was felled after 1488.

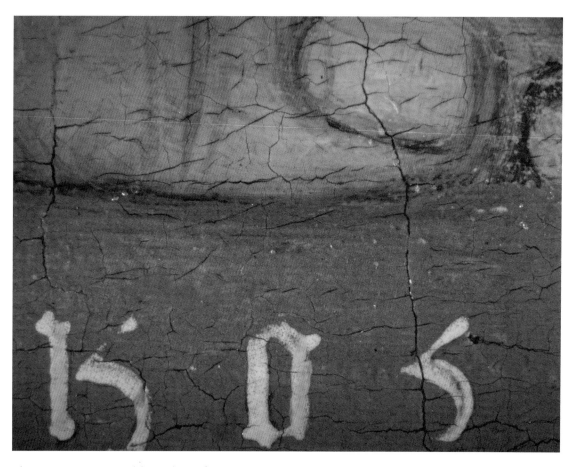

Photomicroscopy can reveal the condition of inscriptions and indicate whether they formed part of the original painting. In this case the brighter yellow areas in the date '1505' are the result of restoration to strengthen the appearance of the numbers; however, there is no evidence that the numbers have been altered during this process.

The inscription at the base of the painting reads: 'Anno 1505 29 octobr[is] jimago henrich VII francieq[ue] reg[is] illustrissimi ordinata p[er] hermanu[m] rinck Ro[manorum] regie [...]' (The year 1505 29 October, the portrait of Henry VII the most illustrious king of France, commissioned by herman rinck, envoy for the king of the Romans). It is quite damaged, particularly in the central section, and the King's name may have been changed from 'henrici anglie' to 'henrich VII' at an early date.

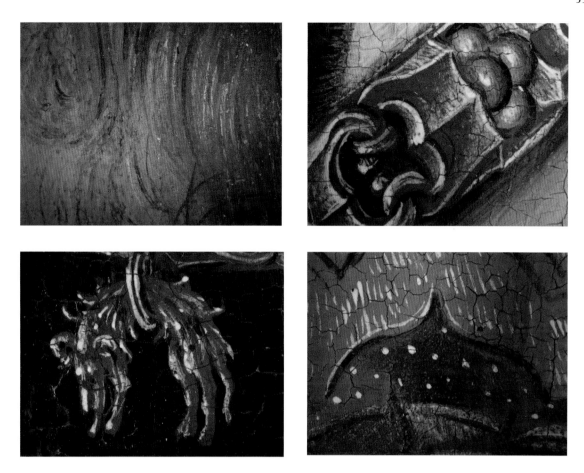

These details of the hair, collar, pendant jewel and cloth-of-gold gown show the artist's attention to rendering the effects of different textures, from velvet to gold and pearls. The pigment lead-tin yellow was used to imitate the gold on the chain, pendant and golden thread of the gown.

HENRY VIII

(1491–1547)

✦

'The Rose both white and Rede
in one rose now dothe grow'

HENRY VIII TIMELINE
(REIGNED 1509–47)

1511
22 February Henry and Katherine's first born son dies at only seven weeks old.

1519
June Elizabeth Blount gives birth to Henry's illegitimate son, Henry Fitzroy.

1502
2 April Henry's older brother Arthur, Prince of Wales, dies suddenly at Ludlow.

Prince Arthur

1516
18 February Katherine of Aragon gives birth to Princess Mary.

1520
7–24 June Peace negotiations with François I of France at the Field of the Cloth of Gold.

1491
28 June Prince Henry is born at Greenwich Palace.

1494
31 October Henry is created Duke of York.

1503
February Henry is created Prince of Wales and Earl of Chester.

1513
16 August Victory at the Battle of the Spurs during Henry's military campaign in France.
9 September English army defeats the Scots at the Battle of Flodden; King James IV of Scotland is killed on the battlefield.

1530
Henry's closest advisor, Cardinal Thomas Wolsey, is accused of high treason but dies before he can be brought to trial.

Cardinal Wolsey

1509
22 April Henry succeeds to the throne as Henry VIII after the death of his father, Henry VII.
11 June Henry marries Katherine of Aragon.
24 June Henry is crowned at Westminster Abbey.

Katherine of Aragon

1533
Act in Restraint of Appeals forbids all appeals to the Pope in Rome on religious or other matters and states that 'this realm of England is an empire'.
25 January Henry officially marries Anne Boleyn.
23 May Henry's marriage to Katherine of Aragon is annulled.
1 June Anne Boleyn is crowned.
7 September Anne Boleyn gives birth to Princess Elizabeth.

Anne Boleyn

1535
6 July Thomas More is executed following his refusal to swear the oath of supremacy and to acknowledge Henry's title as Supreme Head of the Church of England.

1539
Publication of the 'Great Bible', the first authorised edition of the Bible to be printed in English, which is to be set up in every parish church.

Thomas More

1532
15 May The clergy submits to royal authority; Thomas More resigns as Chancellor the following day.

1540
6 January Henry marries Anne of Cleves; the marriage is annulled six months later.
28 July Execution of Thomas Cromwell for treason and heresy; Henry marries Katherine Howard on the same day.

1545
19 July The *Mary Rose* sinks during the Battle of the Solent.

Thomas Cromwell

1534
April Thomas Cromwell is confirmed as Henry's principal secretary and chief minister.
November The Act of Supremacy is passed, establishing Henry VIII as Supreme Head of the Church of England.

1542
13 February Katherine Howard is executed at the Tower of London.

1547
28 January Henry dies at Whitehall Palace; he is later buried in St George's Chapel, Windsor, next to Jane Seymour.

1544
14 September On campaign in France, Henry's troops capture the city of Boulogne.

St George's Chapel

1537
12 October Jane Seymour gives birth to Prince Edward at Hampton Court. She dies only a few days later.

1543
12 July Henry marries Katherine Parr at Hampton Court.

Katherine Parr

1536
Henry begins the dissolution of the monasteries – changing the religious and architectural face of the country.
7 January Katherine of Aragon dies.
19 May Anne Boleyn is executed at the Tower of London.
30 May Henry marries Jane Seymour.
23 July Henry Fitzroy dies.
Autumn A series of linked rebellions against Henry's religious changes, known as the Pilgrimage of Grace, begins in Lincolnshire and the northern counties.

Ruins of Fountains Abbey

HENRY'S PHYSICAL APPEARANCE AND CHARACTER

The young Prince Henry's first major appearance on the public stage was in November 1501, when he led his brother Arthur's wedding procession through London as a ten year old. However, Arthur's death the following year transformed his position and expectations. Henry was subsequently introduced to the court as the heir to the throne, with great success; the Spanish ambassador reported in 1507 that 'there is no finer a youth in the world than the Prince of Wales. He is already taller than his father, and his limbs are of a gigantic size. He is as prudent as is to be expected from a son of Henry VII.'[1]

When Henry acceded to the English throne he was not yet eighteen years old, and as the physical embodiment of the union of the family dynasties of Lancaster and York his reign brought the prospect of long-term security and peace. This was celebrated by John Skelton in a poem for the coronation: 'The Rose both white and Rede / in one rose now dothe grow'.[2]

Henry was a monarch who preferred to execute his responsibilities in conversation rather than in written correspondence, a dynamic young man who contemporaries believed exemplified the virtues of the chivalric prince. A description of his activities whilst on progress around the realm in 1510 described how he exercised himself daily 'in shotyng, singing, dancyng, wrastelyng, casting of the barre, plaiyng at the recorders, flute, virginals, and in setting of songes'; there was also time for jousts and tournaments, hunting, hawking and shooting.[3] He was tall and athletic, described by the Venetian ambassador in 1515 as:

> the handsomest potentate I ever set eyes on; above the usual height, with an extremely fine calf to his leg, his complexion very fair and bright, with auburn hair combed straight in the French fashion; and a round face so very beautiful that it would become a pretty woman.[4]

His character was also seen to be exemplary: the Venetian ambassador went on to describe how the young king was 'so gifted and adorned with mental accomplishments' that he believed him to have few equals in the world. He spoke English, French and Latin, understood Italian well; played almost every instrument; sang and composed fairly and was 'prudent and sage, and free from every vice'.[5] However, those closest to Henry were also aware of his capricious nature; Sir Thomas More counselled a courtier in a Latin poem (here translated) that:

> You often boast to me that you have the king's ear and often have fun with him … This is like having fun with tamed lions – often it is harmless, but just as often there is fear of harm. Often he roars in rage for no known reason, and suddenly the fun becomes fatal.[6]

Reports of his character were discussed across Europe – the Italian statesman and writer

Niccolò Machiavelli described him as 'ricco, feroce, cupido di gloria' (rich, ferocious and thirsting for glory) – as in his hands he held the choice between invading France or making peace.[7] By the 1540s, the break from Rome and Henry's continued anxiety for the future of the realm if he should die before his only son reached maturity meant that this impression had hardened into the image of a dangerous man who was covetous, distrustful and inconstant. The French ambassador reported that his changes to canon law made him 'not only a King to be obeyed, but an idol to be worshipped'.[8]

Henry also underwent a physical transformation over the long years of his reign. Following a number of jousting injuries that left him in constant pain from ulcerous sores on his legs, he changed from a tall, slim athlete into a corpulent man who had to be carried in a chair down the long corridors of Whitehall Palace. This is captured most vividly in the contrast between his suits of armour, which show his chest expanding from 42in. to 57in. and his waist from 35in. to 54in. (figs 15 and 16). It is also clearly evident in the painted portraits that were produced throughout his reign.

These images were intended to project the monarch's power and authority beyond the spaces of the court – not through symbols of rule, but through Henry's physical presence. For the first time in England such images were not simply produced for the pragmatic purpose of dynastic marriage alliances, or for ceremonial spaces, but could also be owned and displayed by courtiers, institutions and ordinary, if wealthy, citizens.

Fig. 15 (*above top*) Foot combat armour of Henry VIII, English, 1520 (Royal Armouries)

Fig. 16 (*above*) Field armour of Henry VIII, Italian, c.1544 (Metropolitan Museum of Art)

THE YOUNG KING

As Henry was a young man when he came to the throne, the image of him that circulated in portraits needed to change as he grew older. This created a singular problem for artists, who would very rarely have been granted a sitting with the King. The search for an appropriate likeness can be seen in a portrait produced in around 1520, when Henry was approaching thirty (fig. 17). In this portrait the preparatory drawing was clearly based on a pattern depicting a man with a much thinner face, with smaller features. The artist then modified the likeness during painting, which implies that he also had another source from which to work, such as a different portrait, or that he may even have seen the King in person at a ceremonial occasion.

In the finished portrait Henry is depicted in his prime. In 1519, the Venetian ambassador reported that 'hearing that King Francis [of France] wore a beard, [Henry] allowed his own to grow, and as it was reddish, he had then got a beard which looked like gold'; the two kings met in a splendid display of ostentatious peace in 1520.[9] Henry is posed in the process of removing a gold ring from the little finger of his right hand. This gesture was frequently used in royal portraits, and the underdrawing suggests that the hands may have been sketched in on the basis of a stock pattern. It may relate to the celebration of marriage but is more likely to refer to the acceptance of the power of kingship or the action of bestowing authority. The King's clothing is particularly lavish, appropriate for a man whom the Venetian ambassador described as the 'best-dressed sovereign in the world'.[10] Clothing was carefully regulated by sumptuary laws, and only the king and his immediate family were permitted to wear the most expensive purple velvet and cloth-of-gold tissue.

At this time, relatively few portraits were produced in England, and it is likely that the painting was commissioned by a high-ranking courtier. This is supported by the comparative expense of the materials used in the painting itself, particularly the gilding in the clothing and jewels. It would also have been surrounded originally by an engaged frame. The frame has been lost, but it would probably have been decorated with bands of gilding and strong colours. This would not only have complemented the colour palette of the painting but also incorporated it into the decorative scheme of the room in which it hung. The painting's heraldic imagery shows the way in which Henry celebrated his identity as a Tudor king: the decorative details in the upper corners (known as spandrels) incorporate the Beaufort portcullis from his grandmother and the joined red and white rose of the Tudors.

One of Henry's first acts as king had been to marry his brother's widow, Katherine of Aragon, and they were jointly crowned on 24 June 1509. A portrait of Katherine, dating

Fig. 17 Henry VIII, by an unknown Anglo–Netherlandish artist, c.1520 (National Portrait Gallery, London)

to around 1520 and of a similar scale to the image of Henry, survives in its original frame in the collection at Lambeth Palace (fig. 18). It also has a background painted to resemble green damask. It is likely that versions of this portrait would have been displayed as a companion to the portrait of Henry during the many years in which they ruled the country as king and queen. Ultimately, the pressure to produce an heir and secure the future of the dynasty led Henry to question the legitimacy of their marriage and to seek to have it annulled. However, Katherine never accepted the title of 'Princess Dowager', always referring to herself as queen, and an inventory taken after her death poignantly records that she retained a paired image of herself and Henry among her possessions.[11]

Fig. 18 (*above*) Katherine of Aragon, by an unknown Anglo–Netherlandish artist, *c*.1520s (Lambeth Palace)

Fig. 19 (*opposite*) Henry VIII, by Lucas Horenbout, 1526–7 (The Royal Collection)

THE KING'S IMAGE

The portraits of Henry that date from the 1530s broadly share the features of the King that were captured in 1520, particularly the small eyes and mouth with a long, narrow nose, and the reddish-brown beard that he wore permanently from 1535. However, the costume and poses are distinct, and it is likely that they evolved from a number of images in circulation that would have been made following a sitting with the King, such as miniatures by the court artist Lucas Horenbout (fig. 19).

The freedom with which the most skilful artists could create portraits from such source images can be seen in the work of the Netherlandish artist Joos van Cleve. It does not seem that he ever travelled to England, but he produced a portrait of Henry while working at the French court, probably using a drawing as a source (fig. 20). A similar portrait of François I was produced by the same artist, and a version was sent to Henry as a gift (fig. 21). The portrait may be the source for the inclusion of a cast shadow

in many portraits of Henry, which creates a sense of a realistic physical space. However, the works produced in England frequently make the error of placing the shadow cast by the King's cap at an impossible angle.

The rupture caused by Henry's break from the Catholic Church in Rome, and the subsequent annulment of his marriage to Katherine of Aragon and marriage to Anne Boleyn, divided the country. Although a comparatively large number of portraits of the King survive from this period, these are likely to represent only a fraction of those that were made as many will have been lost over time. It is possible that the ongoing political stresses created an environment in which portraits could act as a simple means for wealthy subjects to display their loyalty to the king: men such as Henry VIII's chaplain Anthony de Bellasis, who benefited from the dissolution of Newburgh Priory and may have owned the portrait of Henry in a broad golden doublet that survives in the National Portrait Gallery's collection (fig. 22).

Whatever the reason for the increased demand for portraits, it was served by numerous artists' workshops, which produced images of the King for general sale, scaled to the correct size and ready for display within

Fig. 20 (*opposite*) Henry VIII, by Joos van Cleve, *c*.1530–5 (The Royal Collection)

Fig. 21 (*above right*) François I, after Joos van Cleve, *c*.1530 (The Royal Collection)

Fig. 22 (*right*) Henry VIII, by an unknown Anglo–Netherlandish artist, 1535–40 (National Portrait Gallery, London)

Fig. 23 (*left*) Henry VIII, by an unknown Anglo–Netherlandish artist, 1535–40 (National Portrait Gallery, London)

Fig. 24 (*opposite, above*) Henry VIII, by an unknown Anglo–Netherlandish artist, 1535–40 (Art Gallery of New South Wales)

Fig. 25 (*opposite, below*) Henry VIII, by an unknown Anglo–Netherlandish artist, 1535–40 (Society of Antiquaries)

Fig. 26 (*opposite, far right, above*) A distinctive 'dab and twist' technique was used to manipulate the paint in the collar in the National Portrait Gallery's version.

Fig. 27 (*opposite, far right, below*) The fine hairs of the fur collar and beard show delicate wet-in-wet blending of the paint in the National Portrait Gallery's version.

an engaged frame. A clear example of these types of images can be found in three surviving depictions of Henry wearing a red velvet doublet and a fur-collared gown (figs 23, 24, 25). These vary in size but share many characteristics and clearly derive from the same pattern. Although produced for a broader market and made using fewer costly materials – such as earth pigments instead of azurite and red lake in the costume – the paintings were nonetheless skilfully executed. For example, close examination of the National Portrait Gallery's version of the image shows subtle variation in texture in the depiction of the beard and the edge of the fur on the gown, while the dabbing technique used in the collar of the King's chemise skilfully evokes the delicacy

of the fabric (figs 26 and 27). After watching Henry play tennis, the Venetian ambassador described how it was 'the prettiest thing in the world to see him play; his fair skin glowing through a shirt of the finest texture'.[12]

The influence of Netherlandish painting techniques can clearly be seen in these paintings. A number of artists came to England from the Netherlands, and collaborative working practices encouraged the transfer of techniques between émigré painters and native English artists. The practice of creating multiple versions of the same portrait also meant that artists were able to develop and refine their skills.

HOLBEIN AND HENRY

As the 'King's Painter', the German artist Hans Holbein the Younger was paid the comparatively large sum of £30 per year and undertook various types of work at the English court, from decorative painting for court ceremonies to designs for goldsmiths' work. In this role he executed relatively few portraits, but those that he did were recognised as outstanding examples, such as the portraits of Christina of Denmark (fig. 28) and Anne of Cleves that were commissioned as part of marriage negotiations.

Although only two surviving images of Henry VIII by Holbein survive, his depiction of the King became the standard likeness. The first of these portraits was a small painting on panel, which was probably made as a diplomatic gift (fig. 29). The use of the expensive pigment ultramarine to render the strong colour of the blue background, rather than azurite or smalt, suggests that the painting was a prestigious commission, and it may have had a particularly valuable frame. The King's lavish costume is captured in detail: from the embroidered golden collar of his shirt to the golden 'H's in the chain around his neck and the soft white feathers that edge his hat.

The other known portrait of Henry by Holbein was of an entirely different magnitude. Commissioned to cover a wall in Whitehall Palace, probably in the privy chamber, this image of the King provided the focal point for a dynastic mural that celebrated the Tudor

Fig. 28 (*above*) Christina of Denmark, by Hans Holbein the Younger, 1538 (The National Gallery)

Fig. 29 (*opposite*) Henry VIII, by Hans Holbein the Younger, *c.*1536–7 (Museo Thyssen-Bornemisza)

genealogy and provided a backdrop to the King's physical presence in the chamber. The preparatory drawing, known as a cartoon, for the left-hand side of this mural survives in the collection of the National Portrait Gallery (fig. 30). It is made from cut-out figures applied to sheets of paper, and the lines of the design were then pricked in order for a copy to be made. As the preparatory cartoon is in such good condition, it seems likely that it was kept as a record and a pricked copy was pounced – a process by which charcoal dust was pushed through the holes in order to transfer the composition to the wall (fig. 31). Henry VIII's head, which closely resembles the likeness captured by Holbein in the small painting, is on a separate sheet of paper that was attached to the larger drawing at the neck. This suggests that Holbein may have experimented with different angles for the face; the choice of the three-quarter view was evidently unsatisfactory, because in the final image Henry was depicted facing the viewer.

The mural was destroyed by fire in 1698, but the full composition is known through a painted copy made in the seventeenth century for Charles II (fig. 32). It incorporated portraits of Henry VII, Elizabeth of York and Jane Seymour, and a central stone altar with Latin text that translates as:

Fig. 30 (*above, left*) Detail of the figure of Henry VIII from the *Whitehall Mural* cartoon, by Hans Holbein the Younger, 1536–7 (National Portrait Gallery, London)

Fig. 31 (*left*) Detail of the shoe on the left, showing the holes pricked along the lines of the pattern.

Fig. 32 (*opposite*) *Henry VII, Elizabeth of York, Henry VIII and Jane Seymour*, by Remigius van Leemput, 1667 (The Royal Collection)

If you find pleasure in seeing fair pictures of heroes
Look then at these! None greater was ever portrayed.
Fierce is the struggle and hot the disputing:
    the question
Does father, does son – or do both –
    the pre-eminence win?
One ever withstood his foes and his
    country's destruction,
Finally giving his people the blessing of peace;
But, born to things greater, the son drove
    out his councils
His ministers worthless, and ever supported
    the just.

And in truth, to this steadfastness Papal
    arrogance yielded
When the sceptre of power was wielded
    by Henry the Eighth,
Under whose reign the true faith was
    restored to the nation
And the doctrines of God began to be
    reverenced with awe.[13]

This portrayal of Henry's powerful physical presence, with his wide stance and direct gaze out to the viewer, became the definitive image of the King.

AFTERLIVES

Comparison of Holbein's full-length portrait of Henry VIII with the smaller portraits from the early 1530s clearly shows why Holbein's image was so compelling. It was an image that fitted the subsequent narrative of Henry's autocratic power, and full-length copies of the portrait were produced soon after the King's death. Dendrochronological analysis suggests that two of these surviving works – the paintings at Petworth House, West Sussex, and in the Walker Art Gallery, Liverpool – date from the 1540s. The Petworth painting includes many details from the Whitehall mural's composition, such as the scallop-shell niche and the rucked carpet (fig. 33). Further copies of the full-length portrait continued to be made into the seventeenth century, and it was evidently well-known enough for the image to be used, in reverse, on the frontispiece to a history play about Henry's reign entitled *When You See Me, You Know Me*, which was probably first performed in 1604 and first published in 1605 (fig. 34).

Holbein's likeness clearly circulated between artists' workshops as a pattern that could also be used in smaller paintings, such as those produced as part of sets for display in long galleries (fig. 35). It seems likely that artists had access to painted copies from which to work, as well as the pattern for the drawing, because the paintings not only replicate the King's facial features but also such details as the 'H' links in the chain and the gold threads of the costume. These later images of Henry were produced in large numbers to celebrate his reign and to show his place within the genealogy of the Tudor monarchs. So potent was this template that even Henry's detractors acknowledged its power; writing during his imprisonment in the early seventeenth century, Sir Walter Ralegh noted that 'if all the pictures and Patternes of a mercilesse prince were lost in the World they might all againe be painted to the life out of the story of this King'.[14]

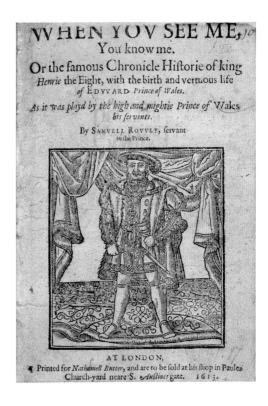

Fig. 33 *(opposite)* Henry VIII, by an unknown artist, 1540s (Petworth House)

Fig. 34 *(right)* Title page to *When You See Me, You Know Me. Or the famous Chronicle Historie of king Henrie the Eight, with the birth and vertuous life of Edward Prince of Wales*, etc. by Samuel Rowley, 1613 (British Library)

SELECT BIBLIOGRAPHY

X. Brooke and D. Crombie, *Henry VIII Revealed: Holbein's Portrait and its Legacy* (Paul Holberton, London, 2003)

S. Foister, *Holbein and England* (Paul Mellon Centre for Studies in British Art, Yale University Press, New Haven and London, 2004)

J.A. Franklin, B. Nurse and P. Tudor-Craig, *Catalogue of Paintings in the Collection of the Society of Antiquaries of London* (Harvey Miller Publishers, Brepols Publishers for the Society of Antiquaries of London, London, 2014)

K. Heard and L. Whitaker, *The Northern Renaissance: Dürer to Holbein* (Royal Collection Publications, London, 2011), pp.64–5, 68

K. Hearn (ed.), *Dynasties: Painting in Tudor and Jacobean England, 1530–1630* (Tate Publishing, London, 1995), pp.40–3

E. Ives, 'Henry VIII (1491–1547)', *Oxford Dictionary of National Biography* (Oxford University Press, 2004), XXVI, pp.522–51

C. Lloyd and S. Thurley, *Henry VIII: Images of a Tudor King* (Phaidon in association with the Historical Royal Palaces Agency, London, 1990)

T.C. String, *Art and Communication in the Reign of Henry VIII* (Ashgate, Aldershot, 2008)
– 'Myth and Memory in Representations of Henry VIII, 1509–2009', T. String and M. Bull, *Tudorism: Historical Imagination and the Appropriation of the Sixteenth Century* (Oxford University Press for the British Academy, Oxford, 2011), pp.201–21

R. Strong, 'Henry VIII', *Tudor & Jacobean Portraits*, National Portrait Gallery, 2 vols (HMSO, London, 1969), I, pp.152–61

NOTES

1 G.A. Bergenroth et al. (eds), *Calendar of Letters, Despatches, and State Papers Relating to the Negotiations Between England and Spain Preserved in the Archives at Simancas and Elsewhere* (*CSPS*), 13 vols (London, 1862–1954), I, no.552, p.439

2 P. Henderson, *The Complete Poems of John Skelton, laureate* (J.M. Dent and Sons, London, 1931), pp.25–6

3 E. Hall, *Chronicle: Containing the History of England, during the Reign of Henry the Fourth and the Succeeding Monarchs, to the End of the Reign of Henry the Eighth* (Printed for J. Johnson et. al., London, 1809), p.515

4 R. Brown (trans. and ed.), *Four Years at the Court of Henry VIII: Selection of Dispatches Written by the Venetian Ambassador Sebastian Giustinian*, 2 vols (Smith, Elder & Co., London, 1854), I, p.86

5 R. Brown (ed.), *Calendar of State Papers Relating to English Affairs, Existing in the Archives of Venice, and In Other Libraries of Northern Italy* (*CSPV*), 38 vols (London, 1864–1947), II, no.614, p.242

6 C.H. Miller, L. Bradner and C.A. Lynch, *The Yale Edition of The Complete Works of St Thomas More*, III.2: 'Latin Poems' (Yale University Press, New Haven and London, 1974), p.205

7 'Letter to Francesco Vettori, 26 August 1513' published in N. Machiavelli, *Tutte le opere*, M. Martelli (ed.), (Sansoni Editore, Florence, 1971), p.1155

8 J. Brewer et. al. (eds), *Letters and Papers, Foreign and Domestic, of the Reign of Henry VIII: Preserved in the Public Record Office, the British Museum, and Elsewhere*, 23 vols (Longman and Roberts, London, 1862–1932), XV, no.954, p.484

9 *CSPV*, II, op. cit., no.1287, p.559

10 Brown, *Four Years …*, op. cit. II, p.313

11 J.G. Nichols, *Inventories of the wardrobes, plate, chapel stuff, etc. of Henry Fitzroy, Duke of Richmond, and of the wardrobe stuff at Baynard's Castle of Katherine, Princess Dowager* (Camden Society, London, 1855), p.38: 'one table peyntid representing the pictours of the King and the Princesse Dowgier'.

12 *CSPV*, II, op. cit., no.1287, p.559

13 G.W. Groos, *The Diary of Baron Waldstein, A Traveller in Elizabethan England* (Thames & Hudson, London, 1981), pp.56–7 for the translation of the inscription.

14 W. Ralegh, *The History of the World* (Walter Burre, London, 1614), f. B1v

Fig 35 Henry VIII, by an unknown artist, late sixteenth century (National Portrait Gallery, London)

HENRY VIII REVEALED

Henry VIII
Unknown Anglo–Netherlandish artist, *c.*1520
Oil on panel, 508 × 381mm
NPG 4690

Detail of the Tudor rose and the Beaufort portcullis
in the decoration at the upper corners. The unpainted
edges of the panel would originally have been covered
by the engaged frame.

X-radiography reveals how thinly the paint was applied
and modelled in the face. The wooden board used to make
the panel support is unusually wide for Baltic oak, and the
line on the left shows where the wood has split apart at
some point and been rejoined.

Infrared reflectography reveals that the initial preparatory drawing that marks out the King's features was much closer to images of the young Henry, or even perhaps his father, Henry VII or his brother Prince Arthur, than the final portrait, which more convincingly depicts the King as he approached the age of thirty.

The painted hands match the preparatory drawing very
closely. Hands composed in a similar way can be seen
in numerous portraits, and it is likely that the artist used
a standard pattern to mark out their position.

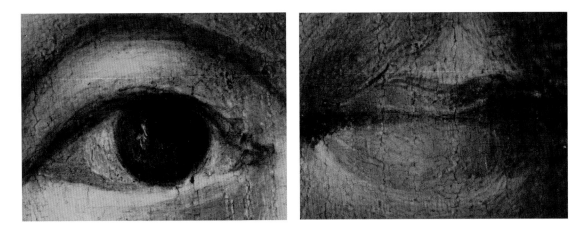

The tinted priming layer, which has an unusual purplish tone, contributes to the dark appearance of some areas of the flesh paint, as can be seen in the photomicrograph details of the eye and lips.

Lavish pigments were used to depict the expensive textiles in the painting, with an azurite glaze applied over red lake to create a rich purple in the sleeves, and large areas of gold leaf.

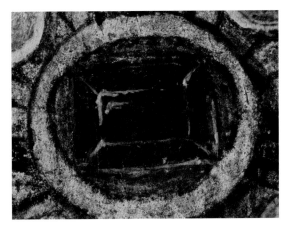

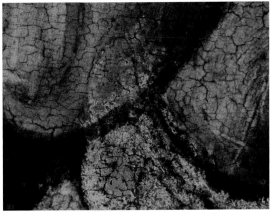

Diamonds set into jewellery were frequently backed with black foil, in order to increase the lustre of the stone. This is reflected in the way in which they are depicted in paintings as black stones, which are cut with a flat top and angled sides.

The gilding for the ring can be seen extending beneath the flesh paint of the fingers and was either applied first, or in the wrong place.

The artist added texture to the depiction of the luxurious damask backdrop by varying the thickness of the paint mixture. The same technique was used to create the small jewels on the collar, where azurite was applied over lead white.

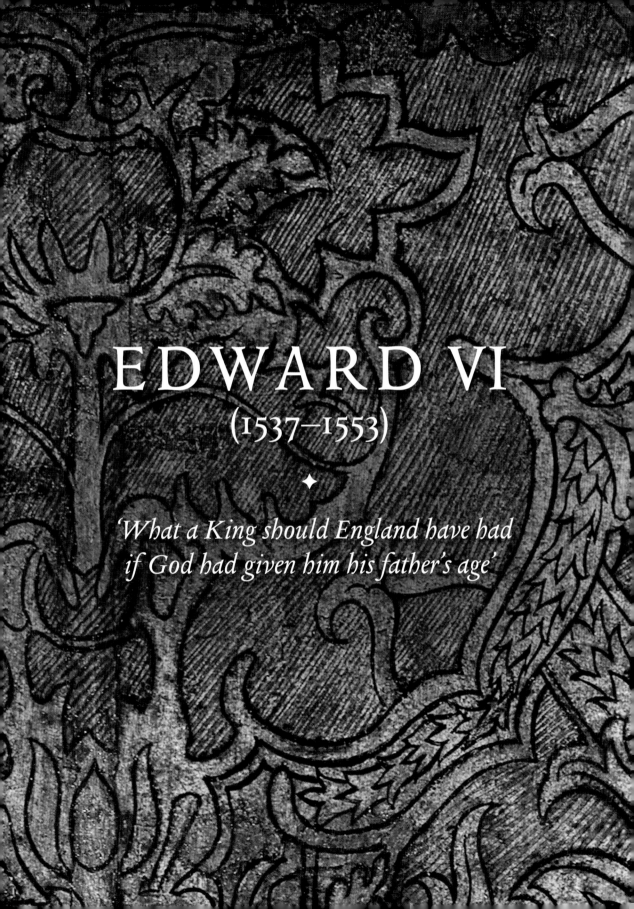

EDWARD VI
(1537–1553)

✦

*'What a King should England have had
if God had given him his father's age'*

EDWARD VI TIMELINE
(REIGNED 1547–53)

Hampton Court Palace

1537
12 October Jane Seymour gives birth to Prince Edward at Hampton Court Palace.
24 October Jane Seymour dies following complications in childbirth.

1543
July Prince Edward is betrothed to Mary, Queen of Scots, then seven months old.

1547
28 January Henry VIII dies and Edward succeeds to the throne as Edward VI under the supervision of a council nominated by Henry.
31 January Edward's councillors recognise his uncle, Edward Seymour, Earl of Hertford, as Lord Protector of the realm and governor of the King's person.
16 February Edward Seymour is made Duke of Somerset.
19 February Edward rides in procession to Westminster Palace from the Tower of London.
20 February Edward is crowned at Westminster Abbey.
May Thomas Seymour, the Duke of Somerset's brother, marries Henry VIII's widow, Katherine Parr.
10 September Victory at the Battle of Pinkie after the Duke of Somerset decides to invade Scotland (which triggers war with France).

Edward Seymour

Coronation procession of Edward VI

Thomas Cranmer

Thomas Seymour

1549
Archbishop Thomas Cranmer produces a uniform service of worship
in English in the first Book of Common Prayer. Its enforcement
prompts armed resistance in the country.
20 March Thomas Seymour is executed on charges of treason.
6 October Duke of Somerset moves Edward to Windsor Castle after
the nobility begin to plot against him for failing to deal with the rebellion.
13 October Duke of Somerset's protectorate is dissolved.

1552
22 January Duke of
Somerset is executed on
trumped-up charges after
conspiring against the
Duke of Northumberland.

1551
11 October John Dudley,
Earl of Warwick, is made
Duke of Northumberland.

1548
28 February
Religious images in
churches are banned.

Detail of iconoclasm from a portrait of Edward VI

1550
2 February John Dudley, Earl of Warwick,
secures Edward's approval for his own
appointment to the office of Lord President.
10 April Duke of Somerset is readmitted
to the Privy Council.

John Dudley

1553
21 May Northumberland's son
Guildford Dudley marries Lady Jane
Grey (who had a claim to the throne
through her descent from Henry
VIII's sister Mary). Edward's
'Devise for the succession' names
Lady Jane Grey as his successor.
6 July Edward VI dies at
Greenwich after falling ill in April.
8 August Edward VI is buried in
Westminster Abbey in an unmarked
grave beneath Torrigiano's altar
for Henry VII's tomb.

EDWARD AS PRINCE AND KING

The death of Katherine of Aragon shortly before the execution of Anne Boleyn ensured that Henry VIII's third marriage could not be challenged. Jane Seymour had been maid of honour to both Katherine and Anne, and the King's interest in her was encouraged by her ambitious brother, Edward Seymour. A little over a year after Henry and Jane's marriage, she gave birth to the longed-for prince, Edward, but following complications in childbirth she died a few days later.

Edward's birth meant that the King finally had a legitimate male heir, his 'moost noble and moost precyous joyelle [jewel]'.[1] Henry clearly delighted in the infant; on one occasion it was reported that he had spent the day with the Prince 'with much mirth and joy, dallying with him in his arms a long space, and so holding him in a window to the sight and comfort of all'.[2] The country's hopes for the boy were captured in a portrait by Hans Holbein the Younger, which the artist presented to the King as a New Year's gift in 1539 (fig. 36). It contained a prominent Latin inscription composed by the humanist Sir Richard Morison, here translated, exhorting Edward to take up his father's mantle:

Little one, emulate thy father and be the heir of his virtue; the world contains nothing greater … Shouldst thou surpass him, thou has outstript all, nor shall any surpass thee in ages to come.[3]

Henry attempted to secure the stability of his son's position by appointing sixteen executors in his will, whom he wished to form Edward's Privy Council. However, Edward's uncle, Edward Seymour, was appointed Protector barely three days

Fig. 36 Edward VI, by Hans Holbein the Younger, probably 1538 (National Gallery of Art, Washington)

after the old king's death. Edward was only nine years old when he became king. Nonetheless, he was never a simple puppet; his broad humanistic education followed the model set for the ideal Christian prince and prepared him for debate and discourse. Unlike his father, he clearly enjoyed writing. An extraordinary 'Chronicle' written in his own hand survives, which, although often appearing coolly detached, provides unique insight into his reign (fig. 37). His desire to shape the events of the realm is clearly evident in the 'Devise for the succession' that he composed and amended in his last months. This revised his father's instructions by ruling out his half-sisters' claim to the throne, as Mary and Elizabeth were still considered to be illegitimate, in favour of his cousin Jane Grey, the granddaughter of Henry VIII's sister Mary.

In 1553, Girolamo Cardano met the young King and cast his horoscope. The Italian physician and astrologer later wrote that he found Edward to be 'of a stature somewhat below the middle height, pale-faced with grey eyes, a grave aspect, decorous and handsome'.[4] However, despite Cardano's predictions of a long and happy life, Edward was dead within a year, leaving Morison, who had expressed the nation's hopes for the young prince in his verses for Holbein's portrait, to wistfully lament: 'What a King should England have had if God had given him his father's age.'[5]

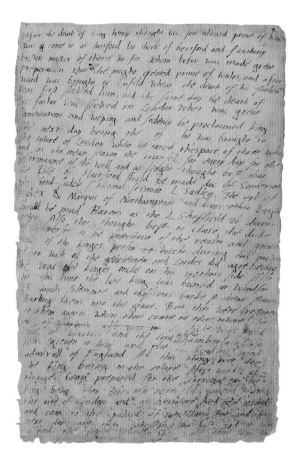

Fig. 37 Page from Edward VI's 'Chronicle', 1547 (British Library)

ENGLAND'S JEWEL

As a legitimate male heir to the throne, Edward's importance meant that numerous portraits of him were commissioned as he grew up. There is therefore a far greater record of his physical appearance in comparison to his half-sisters, Mary and Elizabeth. A few years after presenting Henry with the portrait of his son as an infant, Holbein drew the young boy again, at the age of about five (fig. 38). The artist evidently succeeded in persuading the 'mery' and 'marvelowss plesantly desposed' young boy to sit still[6] – and with its steady frontal gaze the portrait is notably direct.

There is no known painted portrait by Holbein that uses this drawing, and he might not have made one. However, the likeness was used to provide a pattern for the Prince's portrait, which appears to have been quickly shared between artists' workshops. The format was extended to half-length in some versions, to allow for the inclusion of Edward's hands: he holds a red rose and rests his hands on a green cushion (fig. 39). These portraits are all likely to date to a similar period, for unlike images of an older king, such as Henry VII, the pattern would be quickly superseded by another likeness as the Prince grew up.

Childhood was a dangerous time in the sixteenth century; in 1541 Edward caught malaria at Hampton Court, and Henry hurriedly summoned all the doctors in the country. By the following spring, Henry's physician, Dr Butts, reported that Edward 'have prayed me to go away and have called me fool', which perhaps gives a hint of his later stubbornness.[7] The motivation for the production of such images can perhaps, therefore, be found in the desire to present a portrait that showed the future of the dynasty was secure in the figure of a healthy prince.

Fig. 38 (left) Edward VI, by Hans Holbein the Younger, c.1540–2 (The Royal Collection)

Fig. 39 (opposite) Edward VI, after Hans Holbein the Younger, c.1542 (National Portrait Gallery, London)

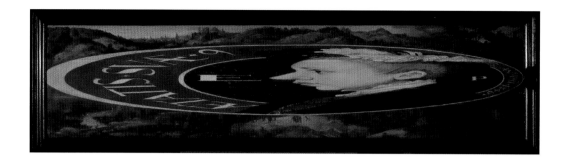

Figs 40 and 41 Edward VI, attributed to Guillim Scrots, 1546 (National Portrait Gallery, London)

THE PRINCE'S PAINTER

One of the most intriguing portraits of Edward was painted in 1546, when he was nine years old. He is shown in distorted perspective (anamorphosis), a technique designed to display the talent of the painter and amaze the spectator (fig. 40). When viewed from a specific point, the features, which appear 'so long and misfired that they do not seem to represent a human being',[8] were resolved into a coin-like portrait suspended in a fantastical landscape (fig. 41). Such technical trickery may well have been used to amuse the young prince.

Very unusually, the painting retains its original engaged frame, which would have been constructed around the panel before the artist began painting. This is probably because a notch in the edge provided the reference point for the correct viewing angle, and the frame also stored the original iron viewing device (now lost) that extended to show the correct position in which to stand. The artist chose to inscribe his name faintly on the frame: 'guilhelmus pingebat' (Guillim painted it). This is now only visible using x-radiography (fig. 42).

By far the most prominent 'Guillim' (or William) working at the English court at this time was the Netherlandish artist Guillim Scrots. He had worked at the Habsburg court in Bruges as a painter to Mary of Hungary, the regent of the Netherlands, and made his way to England in 1545. It was probably as a result of the status of his previous employment that he became the highest-paid artist at the English court, with an annual salary of £62 10s. Edward's likeness in the portrait also exists in numerous half-length versions (fig. 43). These all probably derive from a portrait by Scrots, who would have been the most likely artist to have had access to the Prince. Both the surviving half-length portraits and the anamorphic portraits would have looked very different when they were first produced, because the backgrounds include large quantities of the blue pigment smalt. This

Fig. 42 X-ray detail of the frame on the portrait of Edward, revealing the inscription ('guilhelmus pingebat')

not only fades from a strong royal blue over time but also causes the oil in the paint mixture to discolour to brown.

It is evident that Scrots did not work alone in his production of the anamorphic portrait as the landscape background is clearly the work of another hand. The free handling of the paint in the landscape, with smaller, finer brushstrokes and fluidly blended paint, suggests that the artist may have been a specialist from the Netherlands (figs 44 and 45).

Fig. 43 (*opposite*) Edward VI, by an unknown artist after Guillim Scrots, *c*.1546 (National Portrait Gallery, London)

Figs 44 and 45 (*above*) Details of the landscape background in the anamorphic portrait of Edward VI.

TAKING THE THRONE

An inventory of Whitehall Palace was taken in the year after Henry VIII's death, and among the paintings listed was a 'table with the picture of the whole stature of the kinges Majestie in a gowne like crymsen satten furred withe lusernes [lynx fur]'.[9] This most likely refers to a portrait of Edward, who was then king, painted when he was still a prince (fig. 47). In this skilfully executed image Edward wears a jewel that incorporates a coronet and the Prince of Wales feathers around his neck. It has been cut down on all sides at some point so that the Prince no longer stands at full-length. The painting can be closely associated with a portrait of his half-sister Elizabeth, which features a similarly meticulous depiction of the richest cloth-of-gold. The two paintings are listed next to each other in the inventory, and their wooden panels share wood from the same tree. High-quality companion portraits of this sort would most likely have been commissioned by Henry VIII or his sixth wife, Katherine Parr, who took a keen interest in portraiture.

This depiction of Edward as prince was clearly the source for another portrait, which can be dated to the moment when he became king. It provides a fascinating example of the way in which portrait likenesses and poses could be re-used and reshaped, turning what may well have been a personal royal commission into a more public statement of kingship. In this second portrait Edward again stands holding a dagger in his right

Fig. 46 (*opposite*) Edward VI, associated with the workshop of 'Master John', c.1547 (National Portrait Gallery, London)

Fig. 47 (*above*) Edward VI, attributed to Guillim Scrots, c.1546 (The Royal Collection)

hand, wearing a furred crimson gown (fig. 46). However, in place of the landscape background and fabric cloth, the young King stands before a throne and a more formal golden cloth of estate. The King's arms in the upper-left were added at a late stage. The artist initially intended to have paired windows instead of the column (as can be seen in x-ray), which suggests that Edward became king as the painting was nearing completion. He also wears the golden collar of the Order of the Garter, rather than a chain with the insignia of the Prince of Wales. The underdrawing in the face appears to have been laid out using a pattern, but it is notable that the drawing in the hands is very loose, as if the artist were copying the other version freehand. Similar freehand changes also occurred during the painting process, for although the pose clearly imitates that of Edward's father in the Whitehall mural by Hans Holbein, the position of the young King's right foot has been altered slightly in order to make his stance more plausible for a 9-year-old boy.

Close examination shows that this portrait was the work of more than one hand, with at least three different artists responsible for the figure, the column and the carpet. Such collaboration was typical of sixteenth-century workshop practice. It is possible that the artist known as 'Master John' may have been associated with this studio. Both the portrait of Edward and a portrait of Katherine Parr (see fig. 61), which is attributed to 'Master John', share the very unusual characteristic of a blue preparatory priming layer, rather than the more common grey or pink, which brings luminosity to the sitters' pale complexions.

Another early version of this portrait of Edward survives (fig. 48). The paint handling in this figure appears Netherlandish, and similar to the Royal Collection portrait. Other elements of the composition are much closer to those seen in the National Portrait Gallery version, such as the gilded throne nd cloth of honour. The painting is dated 1547 near the right-hand edge and is executed on a canvas support. Unlike the other two works, the likely date of this picture's production cannot be corroborated through tree-ring analysis. Although few survive, paintings on canvas were produced in the mid-sixteenth century; an inventory taken of the contents of the royal residence of Whitehall Palace in 1542 included a portrait of Edward at around the age of five, described as a 'table with the whole stature of my Lorde Prince his grace stayned vpon cloth'.[10] The three versions of the portrait provide a fascinating example of the ways in which a composition could be reworked for different patrons.

Fig. 48 Edward VI, by an unknown Anglo–Netherlandish workshop, 1547 (Private Collection)

DIPLOMACY IN EUROPE

From birth, Edward's position as heir made him 'the greatest personage in Christendom', and various marriage alliances were proposed throughout his life.[11] The greatest risks to the realm's security were posed by Scotland and France. Thus, after the breakdown of his betrothal to the infant Mary, Queen of Scots, it was reported by the imperial ambassador, Simon Renard, that the English had 'tried to make themselves safe by making proposals, through third persons, for the alliance and marriage of their King and the eldest daughter of France'.[12] Paintings played a key role in these discussions, and a portrait of Edward, which was likely similar to the one that survives in the Louvre (fig. 49), was presented to the French queen, Catherine de' Medici. At the same time, a miniature of Edward's prospective bride, Elizabeth of Valois, was sent to England (fig. 50). Such images utilised to the full the notion that portraits can 'make the absent present', particularly when executed at life-size and full-length.[13] Indeed, the same ambassador later reported that Elizabeth of Valois 'had a portrait of the King placed in her chamber [and] often stands before it, and says to her mother the Queen: "I have wished good-day to the King of England, my lord"'.[14]

It is likely that the artist Guillim Scrots was responsible for the production of this portrait as well as the others that were sent across Europe to support the negotiations, as artists were often commissioned to make multiple versions of portraits at the same time. For example, in March 1551, Scrots was paid for two full-length portraits of Edward, which were destined for Sir Philip Hoby and Sir John Mason, ambassadors to the courts of the emperor Charles V and Henry II of France.

Fig. 49 (*opposite*) Edward VI, attributed to Guillim Scrots, *c.*1550 (Musée du Louvre)

Fig. 50 (*left*) Elizabeth of Valois, by François Clouet, *c.*1549 (The Royal Collection)

AFTERLIVES

Edward's legacy was the establishment of the Protestant Church in England, which was ultimately reconstituted in the reign of Elizabeth I after Mary I's Roman Catholic restoration. The Book of Common Prayer was issued in 1549, and numerous editions of the Bible were published throughout the reign. Edward's authorisation of a revised edition of William Tyndale's translation of the New Testament in 1552 was recorded with an engraved portrait of the King on the title page (fig. 51). This image was re-used in later editions, published in 1566 and 1605 – firmly establishing Edward's role in English reform in the mind of the Protestant reader.

Edward attempted to secure the continuation of the Reformation in England by naming his cousin Lady Jane Grey as heir to the throne. She was viewed as his spiritual successor, and it was hoped that she would provide a number of Protestant 'heirs male' to carry on the programme of reform.[15] However, after her short reign, the upheavals of Mary's reign and the compromise at the heart of Elizabeth's religious settlement, it was not until the publication of the extended edition of John Foxe's *Actes and Monuments* in 1570, commonly known as 'Foxe's Book of Martyrs', that Edward's reputation was secured (fig. 52). Foxe reminded the reader:

how much then are we Englishe men bound, not to forget our duetie to kyng Edward, a Prince, although but tender in yeares, yet for hys sage and mature rypenes in wytte and all princely ornamentes, as I see but few to whom he may not bee equall, so agayne I see not many to whom he may not iustly be preferred.[16]

Edward's reforming role, particularly in the dissemination of the scriptures in English, is perhaps most intriguingly celebrated in a group portrait produced during Elizabeth's reign (fig. 53). This rare survival shows Edward seated on a throne between his dying father and his councillors – the standing figure is probably his uncle, Edward Seymour, Duke of Somerset, and the cleric seated in the centre is Thomas Cranmer. Beneath his feet an open Bible proclaims 'THE WORDE OF [THE] LORD ENDURET[H] FOREVER'[17] and crushes a pope. A scene of iconoclastic destruction is depicted in the upper-right corner, and the surface of the picture is covered with white squares, which were probably intended to contain text. There is, however, no evidence that the texts were ever completed.

Although the composition would seem to suggest that the painting dates to Edward's reign, and particularly to the articles that ordered the removal and destruction of all imagery in churches, the bedridden figure of Henry VIII and

Fig. 51 Title page to William Tyndale's translation of the New Testament, London, 1552 (American Bible Society)

The newe Testament

of our Sauiour Iesu Christe. Faythfully translated out of the Greke.

Wyth the Notes and expositions of the darke places therein.

Viuat *Rex.*

Mathew. xiij f.
Vnio, quem præcepit emi seruator Iesus,
Hic situs est, debet non aliunde peti.

The pearle, which Christ comaunded to be bought
Is here to be founde, not elles to be sought.

printed ult°. Edi: C.th by
Richard Jugg . Anno xli
1552

Fig. 52 *A description of Master Latimer, preaching before King Edward the sixth, in the preaching place at Westminster,* by an unknown artist, late sixteenth century (National Portrait Gallery, London)

Fig. 53 Edward VI and the Pope, by an unknown
artist, c.1575 (National Portrait Gallery, London)

the scene in the upper-right are based
on prints after Maarten van Heemskerck,
which were made in the 1560s.

   Dendrochronological analysis shows
that the panel is made from a tree that was
felled between 1574 and 1590. The painting
may well have been commissioned in
defiance of Pope Pius V's excommunication
of Elizabeth I in 1570 by the papal bull
'Regnans in excelsis', which released her
subjects from their allegiance. As John Foxe
noted in the first edition of *Actes and Monuments*,
while Henry VIII had only 'crakd the Popes
crown', Edward completed his father's
break from the church in Rome.[18]

Fig. 54 Detail of Edward VI and the Pope,
showing iconoclasm.

SELECT BIBLIOGRAPHY

M. Aston, *The King's Bedpost: Reformation and Iconography in a Tudor Group Portrait* (Cambridge University Press, 1993)

K. Hearn (ed.), *Dynasties: Painting in Tudor and Jacobean England 1530–1630* (Tate Publishing, London, 1995), pp.49–50

D. Hoak, 'Edward VI (1537–1553)', *Oxford Dictionary of National Biography* (Oxford University Press, 2004), XVII, pp.861–72

D. Howarth, *Images of Rule: Art and Politics in the English Renaissance, 1485–1649* (Macmillan, Basingstoke, 1997)

O. Millar, *Tudor, Stuart and Early Georgian Pictures in the Royal Collection*, 2 vols (Phaidon Press, London, 1963), I, pp.64–5

R. Strong, 'Edward VI', *Tudor & Jacobean Portraits*, National Portrait Gallery, 2 vols (HMSO, London, 1969), I, pp.87–94

NOTES

1 J.G. Nichols, *Literary Remains of King Edward the Sixth*, 2 vols (Roxburghe Club, London, 1857), I, p.xxviii

2 Bergenroth et al., *L&P*, XIII, pt 1, no. 1011, p.372

3 K. Hearn (ed.), *Dynasties: Painting in Tudor and Jacobean England 1530–1630* (Tate Publishing, London, 1995), p.41

4 Nichols, *Literary Remains*, op. cit., p.ccxv, note b

5 C. Skidmore, *Edward VI: The Lost King of England* (Phoenix, London, 2008), p.261

6 Nichols, *Literary Remains*, op. cit., pp.xxxvii– xxxviii

7 *L&P* Addenda, I, pt 2, no. 1535, p.523

8 L. von Wedel, 'Journey through England and Scotland, 1584 and 1585', *Transactions of the Royal Historical Society*, new series, IX (1895), p.25

9 D. Starkey (ed.), *The Inventory of King Henry VIII*, vol. I: *The Transcript* (Harvey Miller for the Society of Antiquaries of London, 1998), no.10718, p.240

10 M. Hayward (ed.), *The 1542 Inventory of Whitehall: The Palace and its Keeper*, 2 vols (Illuminata Publishers for the Society of Antiquaries of London, 2004), II: *The Transcripts*, no.710, p.91

11 *L&P*, XXI, pt 1, no.8, p.4

12 *Calendar of Letters, Despatches, and State Papers, Relating to the Negotiations between England and Spain: preserved in the archives at Simancas and Elsewhere*, (*CSPS*) 13 vols. (London, 1862–1954), X, p.171

13 Leon Battista Alberti (trans. Cecil Greyson), *On Painting and On Sculpture: The Latin Texts of De Pictura and De Statua* (Phaidon Press, London, 1972), p.61

14 *CSPS*, X, op. cit., p.250

15 Inner Temple, Petyt MS 538, vol. 47, f. 317

16 J. Foxe, *Actes and Monuments* (John Day, London, 1570), Book 9, p.1521

17 This is an extract from 1 Peter 1:25: But the word of the Lord endureth for ever. And this is the word which by the gospel is preached unto you.

18 J. Foxe, *Actes and Monuments* (John Day, London, 1563), Book 4, p.740

EDWARD VI REVEALED

Edward VI
Workshop associated
with 'Master John',
c.1547
Oil on panel, 1556×813mm
NPG 5511

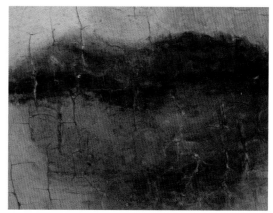

An image captured using infrared reflectography shows the fine lines of preparatory drawing in the face (left). These were followed closely during painting and can be seen faintly through the surface, particularly in the lips (above).

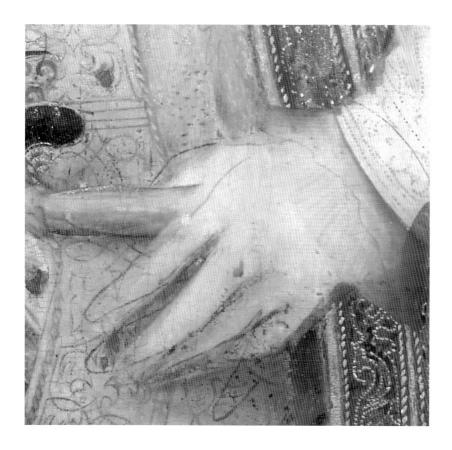

The underdrawing in the hand is much freer than that seen in the face, and the position of the fingers has been altered in the final painting.

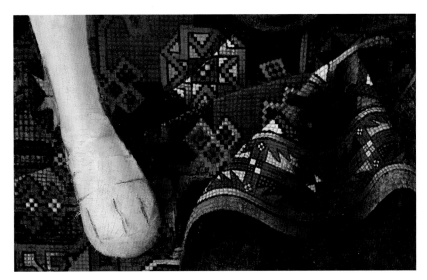

The painting technique varies between different sections
of the composition, which suggests that the portrait is the
work of a group of artists within one workshop.

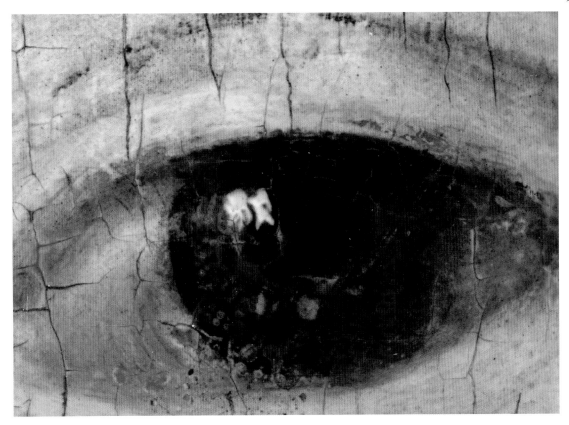

Closer examination using a microscope reveals more details about the differences in technique. For example, the contrast between the tight handling of the paint used to depict the carpet (above left) and the fluid brushstrokes of the grotesque figure at the base of the column (above right) suggests these details are by different artists from the one who painted the portrait of Edward in the centre.

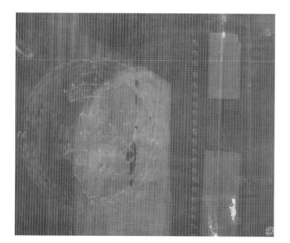

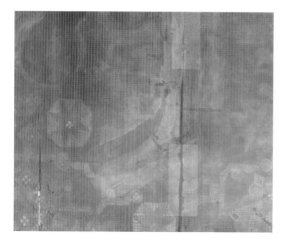

X-radiography reveals that changes to the composition occurred during painting. An arched window was originally planned for the left side, mirroring the window on the right (above, top left). However, in the finished painting this area was covered by the column and coat of arms at a late stage in the painting process. This suggests that the portrait was completed as Edward became king. The second x-ray detail shows that the position of Edward's foot has also been altered (above, bottom left). In imitation of Henry VIII's pose in Holbein's portrait, Edward had originally been placed with his feet in a heroic wide stance; however, this was altered to one more suitable for a 9-year-old boy.

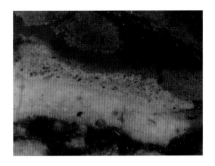

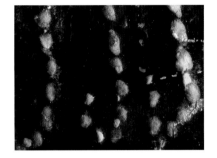

Photomicroscopy shows the lavish pigments and materials that were used, including an unusual blue-tinted layer containing azurite in the priming, which gives the flesh a cool tone. Silver leaf has been used in a double layer beneath the red lake of the crimson gown. The costume, cloth and golden throne have all been gilded in areas.

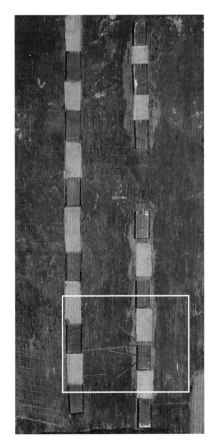
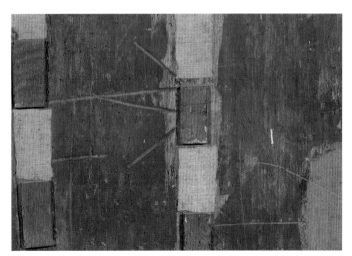

The panel support is constructed from three boards, and the joins have been reinforced with wooden blocks. Tool marks show how the boards were prepared, and there is also a possible merchant's mark, which was probably carved into the wood when it was shipped to England from the Baltic region, before the picture was painted.

LADY JANE GREY

(1537–1554)

✦

'God and posterity will show me favour'

The Tower of London

LADY JANE GREY TIMELINE
(REIGNED 9 DAYS 1554)

Thomas Seymour

1537
October Lady Jane Grey is born at Bradgate in Leicestershire.

1549
17 January Thomas Seymour is arrested on a charge of treason.

1554
January/February Jane's father, the Duke of Suffolk, takes part in Sir Thomas Wyatt's rebellion against Mary I's planned marriage to Philip II of Spain.
12 February Jane and her husband, Guildford Dudley, are executed.
23 February Henry Grey, Duke of Suffolk, is executed.

1547
February Jane is sent to live in the household of Henry VIII's widow, Katherine Parr, who soon marries Thomas Seymour.

1548
5 September Katherine Parr dies shortly after giving birth.

1553
21 May Jane marries Guildford Dudley, son of John Dudley, Duke of Northumberland.
6 July Edward VI dies.
10 July Jane is proclaimed Queen.
19 July Mary, Edward IV's half-sister, is proclaimed Queen by a number of councillors and other authorities.
3 August Mary enters London in triumph.
22 August John Dudley, Duke of Northumberland, is executed.
13 November Jane, Guildford Dudley and two more of his brothers are tried for treason, alongside Archbishop Thomas Cranmer.

Katherine Parr

John Dudley

THE LADY JANE

As the granddaughter of Mary Tudor, Henry VIII's youngest sister, Lady Jane Grey was named fourth in line to the throne in Henry's will. The King excluded her mother, Frances Grey, from the succession, and also the descendants of his elder sister, Margaret, who were unable to inherit property and lands in England as they had been born in Scotland.

Jane was therefore a valuable pawn but had no expectation of claiming the throne.

It was only Edward VI's determination that his Roman Catholic half-sister Mary should not inherit that suddenly brought Jane to prominence. Edward's 'Devise for the succession' was written in the months before his death. The final amendment passed over his half-sisters Mary and Elizabeth and bequeathed the crown to 'the Lady Jane' and her male heirs (fig. 55). It was probably prompted by Jane's marriage to Guildford Dudley, the son of the Duke of Northumberland as the Duke was effectively ruling the country in his role as Lord President of the Council.

Following Edward's death, it was Northumberland who moved to place Jane on the throne; however, Mary's allies rallied and she was proclaimed Queen only days later. Although condemned for treason, Jane's life was initially spared, but her father's involvement in Sir Thomas Wyatt's rebellion in 1554 sealed her fate.

Even during the uncertain time between Edward's death and Mary's accession, Jane made little mark on contemporary commentators, and given the short period of her reign it is not likely that a portrait was ever produced. The most detailed description of her to survive was made by a Genoese merchant, Battista Spinola, who saw her when she was conducted to the Tower of London following her proclamation as Queen. He noted that she was 'very short and thin, but prettily shaped and graceful. She has small features and a well-made nose … the eyebrows are arched and darker than her hair, which is nearly red'; she also wore high shoes 'to make her look much taller … as she is very small and short'.[1]

As for her character, it is perhaps expressed most clearly in an epigram that she composed shortly before her execution: 'If my faults deserve punishment, my youth at least, and my imprudence were worthy of excuse; God and posterity will show me favour.'[2]

Fig. 55 (opposite) Edward VI's 'Devise for the succession', 1553 (Inner Temple Library)

AFTERLIVES

Highly educated and devoutly Protestant, it was only during Elizabeth I's reign that Jane became more widely known. Roger Ascham praised her erudition in *The Scholemaster*,[3] while John Foxe published the details of her final days in the *Actes and Monuments*, describing her and Guildford as 'two innocentes in comparison of them that sat vpon them', a comment that refers to the Duke of Northumberland and his supporters.[4]

Numerous portraits have been identified as Jane, but no certain image made during her lifetime appears to have survived, if one ever existed. One portrait thought to depict Jane was painted in the Elizabethan period and was probably produced in response to her growing reputation as a Protestant martyr (fig. 56). In this three-quarter-length image, she stands holding a book, wearing a costly, if simply painted, gown of red velvet and cloth-of-gold and silver. Tree-ring dating suggests that the portrait was painted in the 1590s, and thus it may derive from an earlier likeness, or could even have been adapted from a portrait of another sitter. Whatever the case, it is clear that the portrait served as a likeness of Jane for its Elizabethan audience. The fragmentary inscription, which identifies the sitter as 'Lady Jayne', suggests that it may have formed part of a set of portraits, and the scratched lines across the eyes and mouth may be the result of a deliberate attack at some point in its history.

By the seventeenth century a growing interest in antiquarianism prompted the publication of numerous collections of

IANA GRAYA DECOLLATA.
Regia stirps tristi cinxi diademate crines
Regna sed omnipotens hinc meliora dedit
H Holbein inv.   F.V. Wyngaerde ex.

printed portraits of prominent individuals from British history. The image of Lady Jane Grey in the printer Henry Holland's publication, the *Heroologia Anglica* (1620) was stated by the engravers Magdalena and Willem de Passe to be based on a portrait by Hans Holbein the Younger (fig. 57). However, this would not be possible as Holbein died in 1543, when Jane was just six years old. It is likely, therefore, that the original portrait was misidentified as Jane; the jewel at the sitter's neck is very similar to one listed among the possessions of Katherine Parr and so the portrait may be based on an image of Henry VIII's sixth queen. Nonetheless, the inclusion of the image in the *Heroologia* meant that it came to be commonly reproduced as a portrait of England's 'nine days' queen'.

BIBLIOGRAPHY

A. Plowden, 'Lady Jane Grey', *Dictionary of National Biography* (Oxford University Press, 2004), XXIII, pp.856–9

NOTES

1 R. Davey, *The Nine Days' Queen: Lady Jane Grey and Her Times, ed. and with an introduction by Martin Hume* (Methuen, London, 1909), p.253. Davey citing a letter in the Genoese archives.

2. C. Malfatti (ed. and trans.), *The Accession, Coronation and Marriage of Mary Tudor, As Related in Four Manuscripts of the Escorial* (Malfatti, Barcelona, 1955), p.49

3 R. Ascham, *The Scholemaster* (John Day, London, 1570), pp.11v-12

4 J. Foxe, *Actes and Monuments* (John Day, London, 1570), Book 10, p.1623

Fig. 56 (*opposite*) Lady Jane Dudley (née Grey), by an unknown artist, c.1590–1600 (National Portrait Gallery, London)

Fig. 57 (*above*) Lady Jane Dudley (née Grey), by Magdalena de Passe, Willem de Passe, published by Frans van den Wyngaerde (Wijngaerde), 1620 (National Portrait Gallery, London)

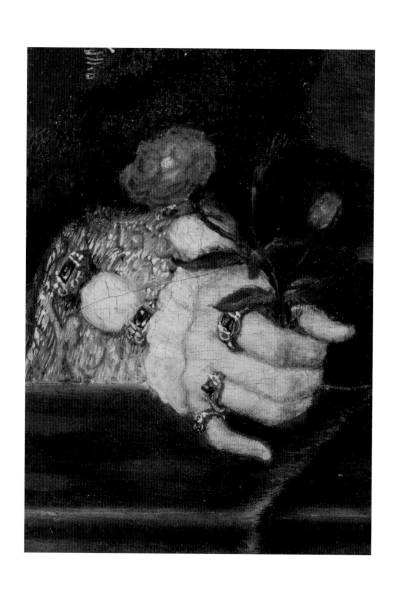

MARY I

(1516–1558)

◆

'A queen, and by the same title a king also'

MARY I TIMELINE
(REIGNED 1553–1558)

1516
18 February Queen
Katherine of Aragon
gives birth to Princess
Mary at Greenwich
Palace.

1527
As part of the
Treaty of Amiens,
Mary is betrothed
to François I's
second son, Henri,
duc d'Orléans.

1531
Katherine of Aragon
is banished from court,
and Mary is forbidden
from seeing her mother.

1534
March The Succession
Act formally declares
Mary illegitimate.

1518
5 October As part of the
Treaty of London, Mary
is betrothed to the infant
François, dauphin of France,
in order to seal a new
alliance with France and
a general European peace.

1523
Spanish humanist Juan Luis
Vives is invited to England
by Katherine of Aragon and
writes a treatise on the general
education of women, *De
institutione feminae Christianae.*

1533
25 January Henry VIII
(officially) marries
Anne Boleyn.

1536
7 January Katherine
of Aragon dies.
19 May Anne Boleyn
is executed.
22 June Mary gives in to
pressure and acknowledges
the invalidity of her
mother's marriage and
the King's supremacy.

1521
Treaty of Bruges provides
for the future marriage
of Mary and her cousin
the Holy Roman Emperor,
Charles V.

Anne Boleyn

Katherine of Aragon

Charles V

Guildhall

1554
January Rebellion led by Sir Thomas Wyatt rises in Kent.
1 February Mary's speech at the Guildhall gains the support of the City of London.
12 February Lady Jane Grey is executed
18 March Princess Elizabeth is placed in the Tower of London.
19 July Philip II arrives in England.
25 July Mary and Phillip marry in Winchester Cathedral.
November Cardinal Reginald Pole returns to England and reconciles the realm to the papacy.

Reginald Pole

1556
21 March Archbishop Thomas Cranmer is burnt at the stake.

1543
July Act of Succession is passed by Parliament, restoring Mary's right to the throne, after her half-brother Edward.

1549
Act of Uniformity prompts Mary to resist the new religious policy; she is granted the compromise of being able to hear mass privately.

1558
January Calais is lost to the French.
6 November Mary acknowledges Elizabeth as her heir.
17 November Mary dies and is later buried in the Lady Chapel in Westminster Abbey.

1547
28 January Henry VIII dies and is succeeded by Edward VI.

1557
March Philip II returns to England to plead the case for England's support in Spain's war with France.

1555
Second Statute of Repeal abolishes all legislation passed against the papacy after 1529.
September Philip leaves England.
16 October Bishops Hugh Latimer and Nicholas Ridley are burnt at the stake, following the reinstatement of the fourteenth-century heresy laws.

Hugh Latimer

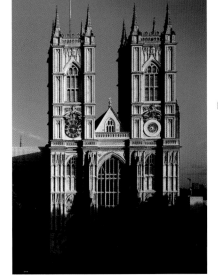
Westminster Abbey

1553
Edward VI's 'Devise for the succession' excludes Mary and Elizabeth from the line of succession.
6 July Edward VI dies; supporters of Lady Jane Grey proclaim her accession to the throne; Mary retreats to Kenninghall in Norfolk.
19 July Mary is proclaimed Queen in London.
3 August Mary triumphantly enters London.
1 October Mary is crowned at Westminster Abbey.
10 October Philip II of Spain's marriage proposal is delivered.
Mary's first Parliament declares the validity of the marriage of Henry VIII and Katherine of Aragon.
First Statute of Repeal reverses all religious legislation passed in Edward VI's reign.

Nicholas Ridley

Fig. 58 (*above*) Mary I, attributed to
Lucas Horenbout (or Hornebolte), c.1525
(National Portrait Gallery, London)

Fig. 59 (*opposite*) Photomicrograph
detail of the jewelled brooch.

AN ELIGIBLE PRINCESS

Mary was never destined to become queen of the realm. Following the disappointment of the birth of a princess rather than a prince, Henry noted to the Venetian ambassador that he and his wife Katherine of Aragon, were 'both young' and that 'if it was a daughter this time, by the grace of God the sons will follow'.[1] As a princess, Mary was schooled to be a royal consort and her marriage would have served to cement diplomatic treaties with either the Valois or Habsburg dynasties. Her early life was characterised by a succession of unrealised betrothals as European alliances shifted. At two years old, Mary was betrothed to the infant heir to the French throne, François, in a lavish ceremony at Greenwich Palace.[2] By 1521, she was betrothed to the Emperor Charles V, her cousin, as part of the Treaty of Bruges. He was sixteen years older than Mary and had the opportunity to meet her when he visited England in 1522 and she was brought before him to dance. A portrait of Mary in miniature survives from the period in which she was linked to Charles V (fig. 58). Prospective brides were often presented with jewels by their future husbands, and in the portrait Mary is depicted wearing a brooch bordered with pearls, with the inscription 'The Empour' (The Emperor) (fig. 59). The portrait is attributed to the Flemish artist Lucas Horenbout, who worked as 'pictor maker' and court miniaturist to Henry VIII, and this image of Mary may be the earliest surviving miniature produced in England.

Charles V broke off his alliance with Mary and married Isabella, daughter of the king of Portugal, in 1525, and Mary was subsequently betrothed to the French king's second son, Henri duc d'Orléans, as part of another Anglo–French treaty in 1527. However, her father refused to allow her to leave the realm as she was only eleven. It was noted that at this age she was 'so thin, spare, and small as to render it impossible for her to be married for the next three years'.[3] By the time this betrothal floundered, Mary's position at court had changed dramatically as a result of Henry's desire to annul his marriage to her mother. She was ultimately declared illegitimate and removed from the line of succession. As a result of her uncertain position, her marriage prospects – to a European suitor or an English courtier – rapidly evaporated. By 1542 these impediments to the prospect of any marriage led Mary to describe herself as the 'unhappiest woman in Christendom'.[4]

THE LADY MARY

The years that followed the annulment of her parents' marriage were marked by Mary's struggle to reaffirm her legitimacy and maintain her Roman Catholic religion. This led to conflict with her father, whom she beseeched 'to consider that I am but a woman, and your child' when she refused to acknowledge the acts of Supremacy and Succession.[5] After Anne Boleyn was recognised as queen in April 1533, Mary had been denied the status of princess and became the 'Lady Mary'. She refused to accept this demotion and endured years of pressure to recognise the invalidity of her mother's marriage and the King's supremacy. However, the execution of Anne Boleyn in 1536 opened the way for reconciliation with her father, and after finally capitulating to his demands she was re-established at court. The last years of Henry's reign were therefore a period of comparative stability in Mary's life; she was restored to the line of succession in 1543 and enjoyed a close relationship with her father's sixth wife, Katherine Parr. A half-length portrait of her aged twenty-eight indicates her rehabilitation in the eyes of the King (fig. 60). The large jewelled pendant that she wears may even be the jewel described as a flower with five great diamonds, two rubies and

an emerald that was given to her by Henry VIII in 1542.[6] The portrait is inscribed 'ANNO DÑI 1544 LADI MARI DOVGHTER TO THE MOST VERTVOVS PRINCE KING HENRI THE EIGHT THE AGE OF XXVIII YERES' and is likely to be the painting for which an artist, known simply as 'John', was paid £5 in November 1544.[7]

The same 'Master John' was probably responsible for a large full-length portrait

Fig. 60 *(opposite)* Mary I, by Master John, 1544 (National Portrait Gallery, London)

Fig. 61 *(above)* Katherine Parr, attributed to Master John, *c.*1545 (National Portrait Gallery, London)

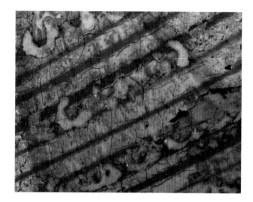

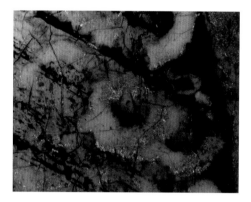

loops of white paint, which were then covered in silver leaf (figs 62 and 63). Such was their value that the wearing of these textiles was restricted by statute to the king and his immediate family, and thus Mary's return to an elevated position at court is clearly shown through her clothes. This was in marked contrast to her years of isolation, when she was regularly forced to request money for even simple items of clothing and personal property.

Following the accession of her half-brother Edward VI, Mary remained resolutely resistant to the programme of Protestant reforms. Her attendance at the Catholic mass was seen as a direct challenge to the King's rule, and in 1551 Edward wrote to her that 'It is a scandalous thing that so high a personage should deny our sovereignty.'[8] Following his death in 1553, Edward's will excluded Mary from taking the crown in favour of Lady Jane Grey, but Mary nonetheless asserted her claim, quickly gaining support from the gentry and nobility. After successfully rallying support in East Anglia and elsewhere and holding her nerve against the Duke of Northumberland's allies, Mary became England's first crowned queen. Aged thirty-seven and unmarried, her triumphant endurance of years of difficulty at court was encapsulated in her new motto: 'Truth, the daughter of time'.

of Katherine Parr that was made at around the same date (fig. 61). The two women shared an interest in fashion, and the clothing that they wear in the two portraits is notably similar, with headdresses (known as French hoods) adorned with pearls covering their hair, and gowns of cloth-of-gold and silver with large cuffs with elaborate undersleeves. Both gowns include the most expensive textile available (known as 'cloth of tissue'), which incorporated large amounts of silk wrapped in gold or silver wire. In both portraits the artist created the pattern of the individual silver threads by painting raised

Figs 62 and 63 Photomicrograph details showing the layered technique and lavish use of gold and silver in the depiction of the cloth of tissue in the portraits of Mary and Katherine Parr.

MARY'S APPEARANCE AND CHARACTER

As a result of her many betrothals, Mary's personal appearance and character were repeatedly commented on by visiting ambassadors to England, with the Venetians noting in 1531 that the 15-year-old princess was 'not very tall, has a pretty face, and is well proportioned, with a very beautiful complexion … [and] she combines every accomplishment'.[9] However, her years of relative isolation, the declaration of her illegitimate status, the death of her mother and the dismissal of her household servants, alongside the failure and then destruction of her marriage prospects, caused her considerable grief and was thought to have contributed to her ill health.

Nonetheless, like her siblings, she was a remarkably determined individual, both sure of herself and proud of her royal lineage, and she learnt how to play her many misfortunes and challenges to her political advantage. Her Roman Catholic faith was deeply felt, and she readily embraced the opportunity to restore Catholicism across the realm after Edward VI's death (fig. 64). This was ultimately put in the hands of Cardinal Reginald Pole, who was made Archbishop of Canterbury after his return to England following years of exile in Italy. Following the burning of high-profile clergymen for heresy, including bishops Hugh Latimer and Nicholas Ridley and Archbishop Thomas Cranmer, and the execution of several hundred others, Mary became incresingly unpopular, particularly in the south-east. To what extent Mary was directly responsible for this policy is difficult for historians to judge; one contemporary commentator

Fig. 64 *The Queen Mary Book of Prayers*, by an unknown artist, *c*.1554 (Westminster Cathedral)

placed the blame firmly with her Council and argued that 'had the executions depended solely on her Majesty's will, not one of them perhaps would have been enforced'.[10]

The most detailed description of her as queen recorded that she had a 'spare and delicate frame, quite unlike her father, who was tall and stout' and that 'her face is well formed, as shown by her features and lineaments, and as seen by her portraits'.[11] Her position as crowned queen was without precendent in England and the transformation of her status during the course of her life was perhaps best captured by Bishop John White in his oration at her funeral, for whilst 'she was a king's daughter … a king's sister … [and] a king's wife', she was the first for whom it would be said: 'she was a queen, and by the same title a king also'. [12]

MARY AS QUEEN

In 1554, only a few months after her coronation, Mary faced the first test of her reign when fears of foreign rule arising from her proposed marriage to Philip II of Spain provoked rebellion in Kent and other areas. She countered these by asserting the precedence of her marriage to the realm in a speech to rally the support of London at the Guildhall. Nonetheless, she was committed to the marriage to Philip, which had been formally proposed on 10 October the previous year and accepted only two weeks later.

That year, Mary sat for her portrait to two highly talented artists: Hans Eworth, a Netherlandish artist resident in England, and Antonis Mor, one of the most accomplished portrait painters in Europe. Several versions of each portrait were produced, and both likenesses became the basis for numerous later copies that preserved Mary's image for posterity. The three-quarter-length portrait of Mary by Hans Eworth shows her standing before a red-velvet cloth of honour, wearing a lavish golden dress with furred sleeves (fig. 65). Her jewels include an elaborate diamond cross at her neck and a large diamond brooch with a pearl pendant at her breast; a reliquary decorated with the Four Evangelists hangs from a chain worn around her waist. Several versions of this portrait survive, and the

Fig. 65 (opposite) Mary I, by Hans Eworth, 1544 (Society of Antiquaries)

image of Mary appears to be somewhat idealised. If the sitting was in early 1554, it is possible that one of these versions made its way to Philip before their marriage. Many years later the imperial envoy Adam von Zwetkowich reported to Maximilian II that Elizabeth I had once recalled how Philip had cursed the flattery of the portrait painters when he first met Mary.[13]

Like Hans Holbein the Younger, Eworth was an artist who was capable of working on a variety of scales. For example, a small portrait on panel clearly derives from the same sitting as that which resulted in the three-quarter-length portrait. In this image, which the artist also inscribed with his monogram and the date 1554, Mary wears a dark, velvet gown with gold brocade undersleeves (fig. 67). Her hands rest on a velvet-covered ledge, and she holds a red rose and a pair of gloves. The different placement of the hands in the two works could have been based on sketches made during the sitting or have derived from standardised patterns. These were further adapted during the painting process when small adjustments were made to the figure.

Later that year a portrait of Mary was commissioned that celebrated her status as a Habsburg consort as much as an English queen (fig. 68). It was commissioned by Philip's father and Mary's cousin, the Emperor Charles V. The artist Anthonis Mor was sent to England from Brussels specifically to undertake the portrait, and he produced

at least three versions, which were probably intended for Charles, Philip and Mary herself. At this point Mary was thought to be pregnant; if the child had been a son, he would have inherited both the throne of England and Philip's lands in the Netherlands. Mary's seated pose, and the choice of artist, ensured that the image would fit within the context of other portraits of Habsburg consorts, while Mor's skill captured a likeness that is perhaps closest to the descriptions of her appearance. The Venetian ambassador noted her wrinkles in 1557, believing that they were 'caused more by anxieties than by age'. He stated that 'her aspect … is very grave … [and] her eyes are so piercing that they inspire, not only respect, but fear'.[14]

A painted portrait of Philip by the Venetian artist Titian had been quickly sent to Mary, with the commentary that 'the picture is already old and therefore will not be as good in colour as the model, who will also have filled out and grown more beard than he had when it was painted'.[15] This painting is lost, but a later copy survives in The Royal Collection (fig. 66). Other, less flattering portraits had evidently been in circulation in England, as the Spanish ambassador was relieved to report that on his arrival in England, Philip 'made a gallant figure on horseback, and the English were greatly pleased with his appearance, because a very different portrayal of him had been supplied for them by the French painters'.[16]

Fig. 66 (*opposite*) Philip II, by an unknown artist after Titian, late sixteenth century (The Royal Collection)

Fig. 67 (*above*) Mary I, by Hans Eworth, 1554 (National Portrait Gallery, London)

Fig. 68 (*opposite*) Mary I, by Anthonis Mor, 1554 (Museo Nacional del Prado)

The portraits of Philip and Mary by Titian and Mor were used as the sources for two small surviving companion portraits produced in 1555 (figs 69 and 70). It is likely that these images were made in multiple versions, possibly as gifts for courtiers both in England and abroad. Mary's marriage to Philip made sense for personal reasons, and when she was thought to have become pregnant soon after their marriage, it seemed as if the Roman Catholic succession was secured. However, it proved to be a phantom pregnancy, and Philip left England shortly after, returning only briefly in 1557 in order to gather support for war against France.

Fig. 69 (*above left*) Philip II, by an unknown artist after Titian, 1555 (National Portrait Gallery, London)

Fig. 70 (*above right*) Mary I, by an unknown artist after Anthonis Mor, 1555 (National Portrait Gallery, London)

Fig. 71 (*opposite*) *Henry VIII enthroned under a canopy on a dais, flanked on each side by his successors; Mary and Philip on the left with Mars behind them, and Elizabeth on the right*, after Lucas de Heere, *c*.1595–1600 (British Museum)

AFTERLIVES

Numerous portraits of Mary I were produced in the Elizabethan period as a part of portrait sets of kings and queens, and these primarily derived from the original portraits by Eworth and Mor made in 1554 (fig. 72). However, beyond this visual legacy, it was the perception of Mary during Elizabeth's reign that did most to shape her reputation as a monarch. If, for historians, Elizabeth was presented as an idealised Protestant virgin queen, Mary was the Roman Catholic ruler who had brought discord to the realm through her marriage to a foreign king. This idea was disseminated most widely in John Foxe's *Actes and Monuments*, first published in 1563, and also in printed images. One such image, produced in the 1590s, was based on a painted allegory of the Tudor succession by the painter and poet Lucas de Heere, in which Henry VIII, enthroned, is flanked by his children (fig. 71). In contrast to the figure of Elizabeth in the foreground, who is accompanied by peace and prosperity, Mary – together with her husband – ushers in war in the figure of Mars to the left. To this image the engraver William Rogers added the verse:

MARY REGYNA ,   ANGLYA ,

Now Prudent Edward dyinge in tender youth
Queen Mary then the Royall Scepter swayd
With foraine blood she matcht and put
  down truth
Which England's glory suddainly decayd
Who brought in war & discord by that deed
Which did in common wealth great sorrow breed

The extent to which Mary's reputation was shaped and overshadowed by her younger sibling is perhaps encapsulated in the fact that she has no royal tomb of her own but is buried beneath Elizabeth's monument with only the inscription (here translated from the Latin), 'partners in throne and grave, here we sleep, Elizabeth and Mary, sisters, in hope of the Resurrection', to record her presence.

SELECT BIBLIOGRAPHY

A. Carter, 'Mary Tudor's Wardrobe', *Costume*, 18, 1984, pp.9–28

J.A. Franklin, B. Nurse and P. Tudor-Craig, *Catalogue of Paintings in the Collection of the Society of Antiquaries of London* (Harvey Miller Publishers, Brepols Publishers for the Society of Antiquaries of London, London, 2014)

C. Hope, 'Titian, Philip II and Mary Tudor', E. Chaney and P. Mack (eds), *England and the Continental Renaissance: Essays in Honour of J.B. Trapp* (Boydell and Brewer, Woodbridge, 1990), pp.53–65

P.G. Matthews, 'Portraits of Philip II of Spain as King of England, *Burlington Magazine*, 142, no. 1162, 2000, pp.3–19

R. Strong, 'Mary I', *Tudor & Jacobean Portraits*, National Portrait Gallery, 2 vols (HMSO, London, 1969), I, pp.207–13

Fig. 72 *(opposite)* Mary I, by an unknown artist, late sixteenth century (National Portrait Gallery, London)

A. Weikel, 'Mary I (1516–58)', *Dictionary of National Biography* (Oxford University Press, 2004), XXXVII, pp.111–24

J. Woodall, 'An Exemplary Consort: Antonis Mor's Portrait of Mary Tudor', *Art History*, 14:2, 1991, pp.192–224

NOTES

1 R. Brown (ed.), *Calendar of state papers and manuscripts, relating to English affairs, existing in the archives and collections of Venice,* (*CSPV*), 38 vols (Longman, Green, Longman, Roberts and Green, London, 1864–1947), II, no.691, p.285

2 *Letters and Papers, Foreign and Domestic, of the Reign of Henry VIII: Preserved in the Public Record Office, the British Museum, and Elsewhere* (*LP*), J. Brewer (ed.), 23 vols. (London, 1862–1932), II, pt 2, no.4481, p.1377

3 *CSPV*, IV, op. cit., no. 105, p.58

4 *LP*, XVII, op. cit., no.371, p.221

5 *LP*, X, op. cit., no.1022, p.424

6 F. Madden, *Privy Purse Expenses of the Princess Mary* (William Pickering, London, 1831), p.176

7 Madden, ibid., p.168

8 *Calendar of Letters, Despatches, and State Papers, Relating to the Negotiations between England and Spain: preserved in the archives at Simancas and Elsewhere* (*CSPS*), 13 vols. (London, 1862–1954), X, pp.209–12

9 *CSPV*, IV, op. cit., no.682, p.288

10 *CSPV*, V, op. cit., no.934, p.533

11 *CSPV*, VI, op. cit., pt 2, no. 884, p.1054

12 J. Strype, *Ecclesiastical Memorials*, 3 vols (Clarendon Press, Oxford, 1822) III, pt 2, p.546

13 V. von Klarwill, *Queen Elizabeth and Some Foreigners,* trans. T.N. Nash (John Lane, London, 1928), p.218

14 *CSPV*, VI, op. cit., pt 2, no. 884, p.1054

15 *CSPS*, XI, op. cit., p.355

16 *CSPS*, XII, op. cit., p.319

Mary I
Hans Eworth, 1554
Oil on panel, 216 × 169mm
NPG 4861

The horizontal woodgrain of the panel is clearly evident in x-ray, as is the broad brushwork in the background, which is made using a paint mix that contains lead (probably lead white) in the grey underlayer beneath the background.

The portrait is painted on a very thin wooden panel, which has been supported at a later date by the addition of an extra cradled panel. As a result, the reverse of the panel is no longer fully visible.

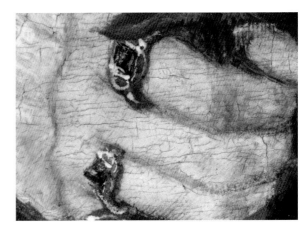

An image captured using infrared reflectography reveals the extensive underdrawing that delineates the composition. The paint layers are very thin, and the underdrawn lines were probably left partly visible deliberately in order to define the features.

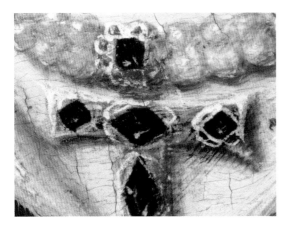

The distinctive jewelled cross with five diamonds is depicted in both the small- and large-scale portraits by Eworth, and was one of the details that was most faithfully replicated in later copies.

The small monogram is quite damaged but reads 'HE' and identifies the artist as Hans Eworth.

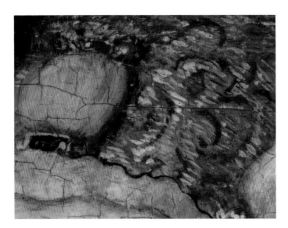

The highlights on the golden cloth in the sleeves and the jewels are made using the pigment lead-tin yellow rather than gilding, thus demonstrating the skill of the artist in imitating gold.

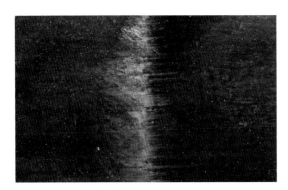

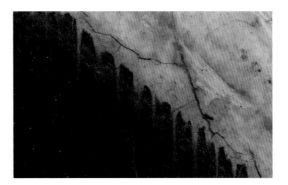

The fine blending techniques evident in the folds of the green cloth of honour and on the edge of the collar helped to create a realistic appearance of the soft edges of the fabric. These marks suggest that the artist used magnification as well as a combed tool to manipulate the paint in creating this picture.

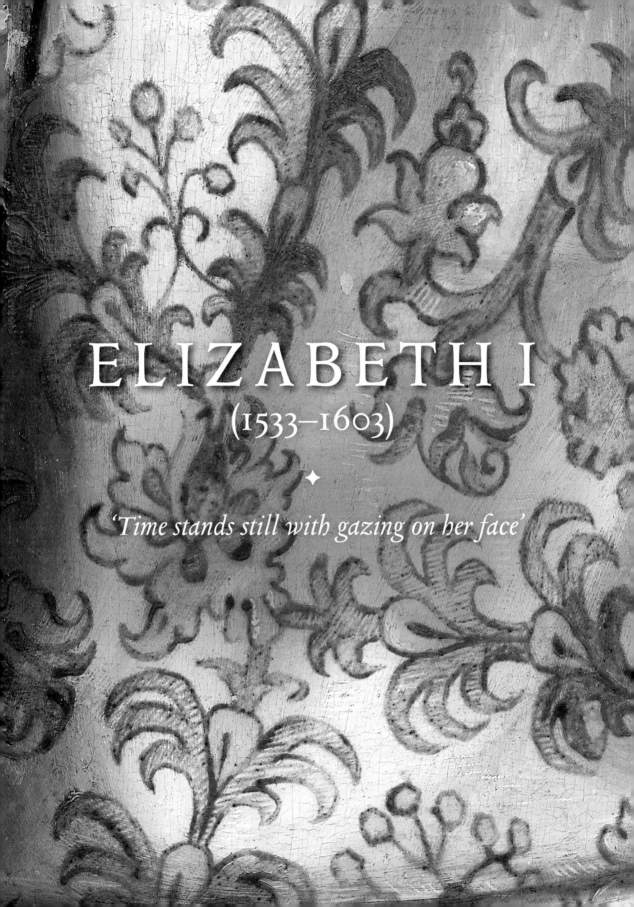

ELIZABETH I

(1533–1603)

✦

'Time stands still with gazing on her face'

ELIZABETH I TIMELINE
(REIGNED 1558–1603)

Anne Boleyn

Thomas Howard

1553
Edward VI's 'Devise for the succession' excludes Elizabeth and her half-sister Mary from the line of succession.
6 July Edward VI dies.
19 July Mary I succeeds to the throne.

1563
The Oath of Supremacy is enforced requiring graduates, schoolmasters and MPs to swear allegiance to the Crown.

1559
15 January Elizabeth is crowned Elizabeth I at Westminster Abbey. Elizabeth announces to parliament that she has no plans to marry. A new Prayer Book is published.

1569
Thomas Howard, Duke of Norfolk (the highest-ranking nobleman of the realm) conspires to marry Mary, Queen of Scots. The northern earls rise in rebellion against Elizabeth's authority, following his arrest.

1533
7 September Anne Boleyn gives birth to Princess Elizabeth at Greenwich Palace.

1547
28 January Henry VIII dies; Elizabeth lives in the household of Katherine Parr.

1536
19 May Anne Boleyn is executed.

1554
18 March Elizabeth is placed in the Tower of London following the Wyatt rebellion.

1567
24 July Mary, Queen of Scots, abdicates in favour of her 1-year-old son, James VI of Scotland (later James I of England and Wales).

Hatfield House

1558
6 November Mary acknowledges Elizabeth as her heir.
17 November Mary I dies and Elizabeth succeeds to the throne. The Queen gives a speech at Hatfield and appoints William Cecil as her Principal Secretary of State.

1570
Pius V issues a papal bull excommunicating Elizabeth. Elizabeth considers marriage to Henri, duc d'Anjou.

1562
October Elizabeth suffers a near-fatal bout of smallpox.

William Cecil

Tilbury Fort

Mary, Queen of Scots

Robert Devereux

Francis Walsingham

1586
The 'Babington plot' to assassinate Elizabeth is uncovered by her principal secretary, Sir Francis Walsingham.

1579
Elizabeth considers marriage with François, duc d'Alençon.

1587
8 February Mary, Queen of Scots is executed following a trial for treason.

1583
Discovery of the 'Throckmorton plot' to place Mary, Queen of Scots on the throne of England.

1588
May The Spanish Armada is launched.
8 August Elizabeth rallies troops at Tilbury following fears of invasion; the Armada is defeated later that month as it is driven north by storms and the English Navy.

1572
2 June The Duke of Norfolk is executed following the 'Ridolfi plot'.

1601
25 February Robert Devereux, Earl of Essex is executed following the failure of a staged rebellion in London.

1585
Elizabeth agrees to send troops to support the Dutch republic against the Spanish.

1596
Poor harvests cause hardship and food riots.

1581
Francis Drake is knighted following his return from circumnavigating the globe. François, duc d'Alençon, arrives in London in an attempt to finalise marriage with Elizabeth and leaves following the failure of negotiations.

1603
24 March Elizabeth dies at Richmond Palace; James I succeeds the throne and adopts the title 'King of Great Britain, France and Ireland'.

1575
Robert Dudley, Earl of Leicester, entertains the Queen at Kenilworth in a final, unsuccessful bid for her hand in marriage.

Francis Drake

Elizabeth's funeral procession

1571
The 'Ridolfi plot' to overthrow the Queen and replace her with Mary, Queen of Scots, is discovered.

Robert Dudley

SUCCESSION AND CHARACTER

Elizabeth I inherited the throne at the age of twenty-five after just over five turbulent years of the reign of her half-sister Mary I. Her mother, Anne Boleyn, had been executed when she was just three years old; she had been declared illegitimate and then later restored to the line of succession by her father, Henry VIII, only to be disinherited again by her half-brother Edward VI and briefly imprisoned by Mary (figs 73, 74 and 75). Elizabeth's unstable early life appears to have had a significant impact on her personality, apparently making her cautious in nature and wary of alliance through marriage. As a survivor of three different royal regimes, by the time she came to the throne, she had developed a seasoned political understanding.

Elizabeth had been brought up in the Protestant faith, and after the unrest and violence during Mary's reign, her belief in a reformed faith was critical to her popularity as queen. As a ruler she surrounded herself with able statesmen and advisers, and together they skilfully brought about the re-establishment of the Church of England to the reluctant acceptance, if not the satisfaction, of both hard-line reformers and conservative factions. Among her many loyal courtiers, her closest and longest-serving adviser was William Cecil, Lord Burghley (later 1st Baron Burghley), who ably guided

the business of government for nearly forty years.

As queen, Elizabeth had an unshakable belief in the divine right of the monarchy and clashed on several occasions with both her councillors and parliament. She was an able scholar who was good at languages, and she also enjoyed hunting, gambling at cards, dancing and playing music. As a person she could be unpredictable, jealous and vain, as well as conciliatory, generous and sincere. Although Elizabeth famously never married and remained a virgin, she enjoyed the company of men and throughout her long reign had several great favourites, including Sir Christopher Hatton, Sir Francis Drake, Sir Walter Ralegh and Robert Devereux, Earl of Essex. However, her greatest affection appears to have been for Robert Dudley, Earl of Leicester, the only one of her favourites to become a serious suitor for her hand in marriage. Elizabeth ultimately recognised that marriage with a subject would prove deeply unpopular. She inspired great loyalty and the culture of the Elizabethan court also allowed able and often attractive men to rise to prominence. Particularly successful were those who played the game of courtly love by championing the Queen's virtues through performances at ceremonial events and tilting contests, poetry, letter-writing and, on occasion, the commissioning of her portrait.

Figs 73, 74 and 75 Henry VIII and Family, by an unknown artist, c.1545 (The Royal Collection) Details of Mary (left) and Elizabeth (right)

PHYSICAL APPEARANCE AND PORTRAITURE

Elizabeth's distinctive appearance – with her red hair, dark eyes and strong nose – is familiar from her best portraits, along with the elaborate jewellery and clothes worn at the height of her reign. As an astute politician she was aware of the symbolic importance of her personal appearance, while as a woman on a public stage she was a keen follower of fashion and attentive to making the most of her looks. In the sixteenth century the very idea of an unmarried female ruler was a contradiction in itself, and there were few precedents or models for Elizabeth to follow. Elizabeth needed to present herself as regal, commanding, wise, scholarly and beautiful, all in clothes and settings that matched her status as queen.

Her physical appearance was commented upon in contemporary descriptions. Most of these accounts were written by foreigners remarking on English court life, such as the Venetian ambassador Giovanni Michiel, who reported in the year before Elizabeth came to the throne that she had 'fine eyes', a face that was 'comely, rather than handsome' and in her person was 'tall and well formed'. He went on to note that 'she prides herself on her father and glories in him; everybody saying that she also resembles him more than the queen [Mary] does; and he therefore always liked her'.[1] In contrast, by her fifties and sixties, it was her use of make-up and a coloured hairpiece that attracted the attention of commentators, and late in life she was described as having a hooked nose, yellow and decayed teeth, a long wrinkled face and false auburn hair, although the writer conceded that her physique was still 'fair and graceful'.[2]

The patrons and artists who were responsible for devising Elizabeth's likeness thus had to invent and adapt appropriate portrait formats during the course of her long reign in order to respond to different circumstances. Her painted image therefore transformed from that of a demure young princess to a beautiful and regal, if rather austere, queen in the 1570s. When it became evident that Elizabeth would remain unmarried and would rule alone, her imagery became increasingly emblematic and allegorical, focusing attention on her unique virtues and the idea of immortality. One interesting early allegorical portrait by Hans Eworth dates from 1569 and shows Elizabeth standing before three mythological goddesses (Juno, Pallas Athena and Venus) (fig. 76). The device was a clever one, which restaged the story of the Judgement of Paris and was designed to offer praise to the Queen by suggesting that she alone combined all the virtues of the goddesses. As the painting was on display in a royal palace in Elizabeth's lifetime, the imagery probably gained royal approval; the same subject is seen in a highly accomplished miniature made more than twenty years later, which suggests that it may have existed in several different compositions (fig. 77).

Fig. 76 *Elizabeth I and the Three Goddesses,*
by Hans Eworth, 1569 (The Royal Collection)

Fig. 77 *Elizabeth I and the Three Goddesses*, attributed to
Isaac Oliver, c.1590 (National Portrait Gallery, London)

In the 1580s, Elizabeth took on the appearance of an elaborately dressed icon at a time when fashions were at their most extreme, and by the 1590s, when she was in her sixties, she appeared as a near mythical fairy queen. Inevitably, as she aged many of her later portraits flattered her appearance. However, in the 1590s the need to re-enforce the stability of the regime meant that it was useful for the Queen to appear continually youthful. Thus the basic outlines of Elizabeth's facial likeness that were devised in the mid-1570s, when she was in her early forties, continued to be used by artists for a further twenty years. This allowed Elizabeth the advantage any film star would envy of fixing the ageing process in time. However, the staging of her court appearances was likely to have been equally as artificial as her likeness in portraiture, as both strove to adhere to the ethos of her motto, *Semper eadem*, 'Always the same'. It was perhaps expressed most clearly in verses of praise set to music by John Dowland in 1603:

Time stands still with gazing on her face.
Stand still and gaze for minutes, hours and
    years to give her place
All other things shall change but she
    remains the same
Till heavens changed have their course and
    Time hath lost his name.[3]

It is clear that the surviving portraits of Elizabeth do not tell the whole story. Many paintings, prints and drawings have been lost over time. Some of the surviving personal inventories of Elizabethan householders show that portraits of the Queen were owned by a variety of people, including merchants and professionals, as a mark of loyalty to the Crown. Furthermore, there is evidence that numerous portraits were destroyed by officials during the reign because they were not considered to do justice to her reputation.[4] In the centuries that followed many other portraits were destroyed both intentionally and through neglect. As extraordinary as it seems today, in one instance in the late seventeenth century, numerous panel paintings of Elizabeth were so ridiculed that they were re-used by bakers as boards on which to bake bread in ovens.[5]

THE YOUNG ELIZABETH

There are very few images depicting Elizabeth as a princess or in the period shortly after coming to the throne. Her earliest surviving portrait shows her at the age of around thirteen, holding a book (probably of prayers) with another, larger book open on a stand behind her (fig. 78). The portrait offers an impression of a serious and scholarly young woman dressed with calculated elegance. Elizabeth is shown in a crimson gown, with wide sleeves, a gold brocaded forepart and undersleeves, of similar design to that seen in a portrait of her stepmother Katherine Parr painted at a similar time. Elizabeth's clothes are obviously expensive and highly fashionable. Hanging within a royal palace, the portrait would have served its purpose as a record of Elizabeth as a demure, dutiful and elegant princess, thereby marking her return to the royal succession. That Elizabeth posed directly for the artist to create this portrait seems apparent from the sharply observed likeness and the meticulously painted details of the costume.

Elizabeth's understanding of portraiture at this time is revealed in a fascinating letter that she sent to her half-brother, Edward VI, probably in 1551, which evidently accompanied a portrait. She beseeched Edward 'that when you shall look on my picture you will witsafe it to think that as you have but the outward shadow of the body afore you, so my inward minde wischeth that the body itself were

oftener in your presence'.[6] Few other certain portraits of Elizabeth as a princess exist, and given her divisive status as the Protestant heir to the throne, it is perhaps easy to understand why. During the reign of her half-sister Mary I, it would not have been politic for Elizabeth to have sat for her likeness; in fact, it was reported that what disquieted Mary most was 'to see the eyes and hearts of the nation already fixed on this lady [Elizabeth] as successor to the Crown'.[7] The production of her portrait would therefore almost certainly have been regarded as a means of generating support for Mary's demise and Elizabeth's future succession.

Fig. 78 (*opposite*) Elizabeth I, attributed to Guillim Scrots, *c*.1546 (The Royal Collection)

EARLY PORTRAITS AS QUEEN

From as early as 1551, the court miniaturist Levina Teerlinc had the opportunity to paint Elizabeth on several occasions. Teerlinc was granted an annual salary and appears to have held a semi-official position at court, indicating that Elizabeth valued her work. In the annual exchange of gifts on New Year's Day, Teerlinc regularly gave Elizabeth a portrait, as in 1559 when she presented 'the Quenis picture finly painted vpon a card', and again in 1562 when the gift was described as 'the Quenis personne and other personages in a boxe finely paynted'.[8] Frustratingly, little of Teerlinc's work appears to have survived, and images attributed to her are naive in style and poorly proportioned.

One portrait, probably produced just after Elizabeth's accession, is a remarkably simple image of the young queen with jewels appropriate to her rank (fig. 79). Elizabeth is recognisable from her auburn hair, narrow nose and dark eyes, but the image has a formulaic quality, indicating that it was not painted from the life but was probably one of many versions (some of which still survive) painted to fulfil a demand for her likeness in the early years of her reign. Technical analysis has shown that the background of the painting has faded dramatically from a striking blue to the yellowish brown seen today. The original yellow inscription 'ELIZABETH REGINA' (Queen Elizabeth) would therefore have once stood out more clearly against the blue background (figs 80 and 81). The design for the head was produced from a drawn pattern, which was probably traced on to the surface and could have been used to create other portraits. Around this date Elizabeth's advisers were particularly anxious about the circulation of poor copies of her portrait, and it is likely that this was exactly the sort of image that would have caused such anxiety. In 1563 a proclamation was drafted, but apparently never issued, that attempted to stop unskilled painters from making copies of the Queen's portrait. The proclamation acknowledged the 'natural desires' of the Queen's subjects to own and display her portrait but stated that no further images should be produced until a suitable original could be made by 'some special cunning painter' taking a likeness directly from the Queen. Such an image could then be copied for replication by many other artists and publicly sold.[9] However, no one prototype portrait of Elizabeth appears to have been produced at this time, perhaps because a suitable artist could not be found.

Fig. 79 (*opposite, above*) Elizabeth I, by an unknown English artist, *c*.1560 (National Portrait Gallery, London)

Figs 80 and 81 (*opposite, below*) Digitally recoloured images to show how the inscription either side of Elizabeth's head would originally have been clearly legible against the blue background.

CORONATION PORTRAIT

A remarkable miniature and a life-size portrait in oil, both of which show Elizabeth in her gold coronation robes (figs 82 and 83), might appear to provide evidence of the type of regal template that was desired by her councillors at the time of the draft proclamation in 1563. However, there are no known copies of the image from the early years of the reign, which indicates that the surviving miniature was probably painted quite some time after the coronation. The coronation robes survived in the royal wardrobe throughout Elizabeth's reign and could well have been used as a source for the image at a later date.

Analysis of the life-size portrait using tree-ring dating has shown that it dates from after 1589.[10] The technique suggests that it was produced in an English workshop, and the composition has probably been copied from an established pattern. Close observation of the paint handling shows the approach is rather schematic and without great attention to detail. This indicates that the image may have been commissioned to accompany a set of portraits or as part of a programme of entertainment or court ritual.

What seems likely is that both the miniature and the painting in oil were produced as part of the regular celebration of the Queen's accession day, which took place annually on 17 November throughout Elizabeth's reign and was marked by celebrations and tilting contests at court. It is probable that other examples of this composition once existed, and the small differences between the two surviving works (particularly in the design of the jewels and the orb) show that they may even have been based on different prototypes.

Fig. 82 *(right)* Elizabeth I, by an unknown English artist, late sixteenth century (Private Collection)

Fig. 83 *(opposite)* Elizabeth I, by an unknown English artist, *c.*1600 (National Portrait Gallery, London)

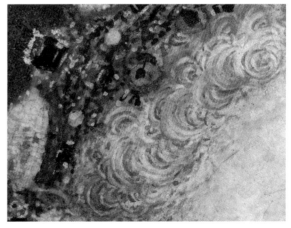

HILLIARD AND ELIZABETH

From the 1570s there is a sense that the Elizabethan regime, and perhaps Elizabeth herself, had begun to take the value of the Queen's image as propaganda more seriously. The employment of the highly talented painter Nicholas Hilliard, who mainly worked as a miniaturist, presented for the first time an opportunity to devise an image of Elizabeth that could serve as a royal icon and be used in official formats, such as on seals for royal documents. Hilliard painted a miniature in 1572 (figs 84, 85 and 86) that shows the Queen at the age of thirty-eight wearing elaborate jewellery and white roses pinned to her shoulder suggestive of high summer. This may be the image to which Hilliard refers in his discourse on painting, 'Treatise Concerning The Arte of Limning', which was written 1598–1603. In this text Hilliard recalled the Queen's views on painting on the first occasion he drew her likeness. She had enquired why Italian artists who 'had the name' to 'draw the best', did not seem to use shadowing in their work, and in order to avoid any shadows in her own portrait she chose to sit for her portrait out of doors 'in the open alley of a goodly garden, where no tree was near'.[11] Hilliard had a meticulous approach to painting, depicting a very high level of detail through layers of linear description. This diagrammatic, rather than painterly, style suited the complex Elizabethan costumes with their layers of different fabrics and the elaborate jewellery

that was worn at court, and became an essential characteristic of Elizabethan court imagery.

The likeness of the Queen's face captured in this small-scale miniature bears a strong similarity to other life-size paintings in oil. It is therefore possible that Hilliard, or his studio, was also responsible for other portraits painted around this date that use a scaled-up version of this 'face pattern'.[12] Two such portraits survive and include carefully chosen emblems, indicating a shift in the way the portraiture of Elizabeth was viewed and understood (figs 87 and 88). The 'Phoenix' and 'Pelican' portraits are named after the two jewels worn at the Queen's breast, and they were almost certainly produced in the same studio at the same time. The two paintings use an identical pattern – used in reverse in the 'Phoenix' portrait – and share characteristic materials and paint-handling techniques; the two panel supports also contain wood from the same trees. The pattern used for Elizabeth's head in the 'Phoenix' portrait was altered in the process of painting, as can be seen from the position of the eyes, which were originally lower in the drawn design (fig. 89). This might indicate that the 'Phoenix' portrait was started first or simply that the artist initially began with the design placed too low.

Fig. 84 (opposite, above) Elizabeth I, by Nicholas Hilliard, 1572 (National Portrait Gallery, London)

Figs 85 and 86 (opposite, below) Detail images taken using a microscope to show the fine detail and skilful paint handling.

The phoenix and pelican jewels were worn as symbols of Elizabeth's virtues and unique nature (figs 87 and 88). A phoenix is an emblem of rebirth and regeneration, and became associated with the Queen in the 1570s, while a pelican symbolises charity as the bird was thought to feed its young by pecking at its own breast to release blood. These jewels probably depict real pendants worn by the Queen, who owned a vast number of elaborate jewels of various designs, often made up of rubies, diamonds and pearls.[13] The 'Phoenix' portrait may once have been in the collection of the dean of Westminster Gabriel Goodman, who had a keen interest in portraiture and owned a number of portraits of Elizabethan courtiers, including William Cecil, Lord Burghley.

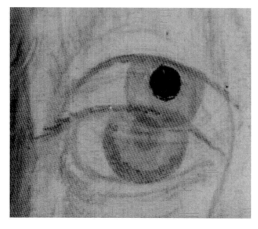

Fig. 87 (*opposite*) Elizabeth I, associated with Nicholas Hilliard, *c*.1575, with detail showing Pelican jewel (Walker Art Gallery)

Fig. 88 (*above*) Elizabeth I, associated with Nicholas Hilliard, *c*.1575, with detail showing Phoenix jewel (National Portrait Gallery, London)

Fig. 89 (*right*) The underpainted eye in the 'Phoenix' portrait revealed using infrared reflectography.

A PORTRAIT FROM LIFE

Elizabeth's early reluctance to sit for portraits – which was perhaps born out of political expediency – may have set a pattern for her lifetime, as she appears to have sat for remarkably few artists. As a result, the majority of the surviving portraits produced in her lifetime are copies and versions of only a few original portraits. The artists who did paint the Queen from life were either royal employees or painters from England and abroad who were specially commissioned by loyal courtiers. For example, the Dutch writer and biographer Karel van Mander noted that, in 1578, Elizabeth I sat to the well-established Netherlandish artist Cornelis Ketel at the request of Edward Seymour, Earl of Hertford, when dining with his mother, the Duchess of Somerset.[14] Sadly, no portrait by Ketel depicting the Queen has been identified, and this work is probably lost. Elizabeth also sat to an unknown French artist in 1581 and almost certainly to her official serjeant painters (in particular George Gower) as well as to the miniaturist Isaac Oliver.[15]

Few paintings of Elizabeth appear to capture her sense of presence and distinctive features as brilliantly as a portrait from the mid-1570s showing her in an embroidered dress holding a feathered fan (fig. 90). Known as the 'Darnley' portrait, after a former owner,

this picture offers one of the most insightful likenesses among all other surviving portraits of the Queen. It shows Elizabeth in her early forties, and her facial features as captured here served as the model for a vast number of other portraits for the next twenty years. It is clear, therefore, that Elizabeth must have approved of this image, which shows her as both a beautiful woman and a powerful regal leader, equal to the male sovereigns of Europe. The artist was clearly a skilled and practised portraitist, and may have been brought to England especially for this commission. Interestingly, the image also serves as an important exemplar of the changes that can occur over the course of a painting's history. Elizabeth herself noted, in regard to an earlier painting that she sent to Edward VI, that 'from the grace of the picture the colours may fade by time'.[16] Technical analysis has shown this observation to be particularly apt in the case of the 'Darnley' portrait, as the red pigments in both the dress and the flesh have faded, and thus Elizabeth's complexion was originally more natural than the pale features seen here.

The portrait was once attributed to Federico Zuccaro, an Italian artist who visited England in 1575 and completed a drawing of Elizabeth in May that year (fig. 91). However, the attribution of the 'Darnley' portrait to Zuccaro is not sustainable, and the paint handling in the picture appears to be more consistent with Netherlandish practice. Technical analysis has shown that the crown in the background is almost certainly by another, less competent artist and may have been added shortly after the painting's completion, perhaps at the request of a patron.

Fig. 90 (*opposite*) Elizabeth I, by an unknown Continental artist, *c*.1575 (National Portrait Gallery, London)

LATE PORTRAITS

Some portraits of the Queen were painted by accomplished artists abroad and imported back into England as commissions from specific courtiers. This may have been the case with a portrait by Marcus Gheeraerts the Elder, dating from the mid-1580s (fig. 92). The artist had been in England for a short period in the later 1560s but was back in Flanders from 1577. He produced a portrait of Elizabeth as an allegorical personification of 'Peace', holding an olive branch with the sword of justice at her feet. In this image, the likeness of the Queen's face is unlikely to have been based on a sitting. The unusual setting, with a doorway opening on to a garden and three figures in the background, would seem to indicate that the composition was directed by a particular patron; the

Fig. 91 (*opposite*) Elizabeth I, by Federico Zuccaro, 1575 (British Museum)

Fig. 92 (*below*) Elizabeth I, by Marcus Gheeraerts the Elder, *c*.1585 (Private Collection)

painting has long been associated with the house of Robert Dudley, Earl of Leicester.

The decades of the 1580s and 1590s saw an increase in demand for the Queen's portrait, probably in response to the threat of invasion from Roman Catholic Spain, which culminated in the attack of the Spanish Armada in 1588. The display of a portrait of Elizabeth may well have demonstrated the owner's loyalty and patriotism, and also their Protestant credentials, at a time when the country was facing foreign hostility. Significant numbers of surviving portraits of Elizabeth use the same basic facial pattern with interchangeable costumes, indicating that these images were produced by a variety of workshops with access to drawn tracings of the Queen's head. One such example (fig. 93), of which many other similar versions exist, shows Elizabeth wearing a heart-shaped pendant and holding a large feathered fan; it dates to 1585–90. Elizabeth would not have sat directly for a portrait of this type; instead the facial likeness is based on a pattern taken from the 'Darnley' portrait, made over ten years previously, which appears to have circulated between artists' workshops.

Following the defeat of the Spanish Armada in 1588, it is unsurprising that newly commissioned portraits celebrated Elizabeth's reputation as a glorious and triumphant leader. There are several surviving versions of the so-called 'Armada portrait',

dating from after 1588 (figs 94, 95 and 96). The composition shows the Queen with her face framed by an enormous lace ruff, bedecked in diamonds, rubies and pearls with her hand upon a globe, as if empress of the world. The scenes from the windows in the background show the English ships, on the left, and, to the right, the Spanish ships foundering on the coast. Close comparison of these three surviving paintings clearly indicates they were produced in different workshops. It is probable that this composition was replicated in multiple versions that no longer survive.

One of the few convincing images showing the Queen as she looked as an older woman is a remarkable unfinished miniature by Isaac Oliver (fig. 97). The likeness appears to be taken from the life as Elizabeth's features, such as her heavy-lidded eyes and strong nose, are very carefully observed. It is quite possible that the image was not completed because it was considered too realistic; however, the face pattern seen here was employed after her death in printed sources, when there was no need for her image to be policed. In contrast to this insightful likeness, various printed portraits of the Queen were produced for wider dissemination throughout her reign and may have been quite widely available; however, only a few examples survive today. A large-scale woodcut, dating c.1590 (fig. 98), shows how Elizabeth would have been seen by a wide audience, holding the traditional symbols of monarchy: the sceptre and orb. The print would have been cheap to produce, and such examples were pasted in books or

Fig. 93 Elizabeth I, by an unknown artist, c.1585–90 (National Portrait Gallery, London)

Fig. 94 Elizabeth I, by an unknown English artist,
c.1588 (Woburn Abbey)

Fig. 95 Elizabeth I, by an unknown English artist,
c.1588 (Tyrwhitt-Drake Collection)

Fig. 96 (*opposite*) Elizabeth I, by an unknown English artist, *c.*1588 (National Portrait Gallery, London)

Fig. 97 (*above*) Elizabeth I, by Isaac Oliver, 1590–2 (Victoria and Albert Museum)

pinned up in homes to allow the citizenry to display a portrait of their queen.

Perhaps the most remarkable portrait depicting the Queen in later life is the so-called 'Ditchley' portrait, which shows her standing on a globe (fig. 99). Her feet rest on Oxfordshire, where the courtier Sir Henry Lee staged an elaborate programme of entertainment for Elizabeth at his house at Ditchley in 1592. Lee had served as the 'Queen's Champion' between 1571 and 1590, a role that involved masterminding the complex accession-day celebrations. He was therefore a past master at devising court entertainments, and the painting probably played a part in the staged events. The text to the right refers to the Queen as the 'prince of light' and may have been read aloud as part of the entertainment. Elizabeth is shown turning away from stormy skies, a gesture that may celebrate her forgiveness of Sir Henry Lee, whose misdemeanour had been to live with his mistress following his retirement. The painting is attributed to Marcus Gheeraerts the Younger, a Netherlandish artist who is known to have worked for Lee.

Fig. 98 (*above*) *Elizabetha Regina*, by an unknown artist, late sixteenth century (Ashmolean Museum)

Fig. 99 (*opposite*) Elizabeth I, by Marcus Gheeraerts the Younger, *c.*1592 (National Portrait Gallery, London)

AFTERLIVES

There continued to be a lively demand for Elizabeth's likeness after her death, and such images often took their place in portrait sets presenting a visual chronology of British history. The strength of Elizabeth's visual legacy is perhaps best encapsulated in the title of Thomas Heywood's play *If you know not me, You know no bodie: Or, The troubles of Queene Elizabeth*, which was published in fourteen editions between 1605 and 1633. This deliberately referenced Samuel Rowley's chronicle of Henry VIII's reign, *When you see me, You know me*, which had been published in 1605. The frontispiece included an image of Elizabeth enthroned, familiar, as with the image of her father, from her silhouette (fig. 100).

Incredibly, Elizabeth's accession day went on being celebrated into the eighteenth century as a national holiday, and images of the Queen (then seen as a great, patriotic Protestant champion), were evidently still in demand. However, the painting style of the Elizabethan period did not enjoy the same level of appreciation in later centuries. This resulted in the creation of fascinating hybrid images, in which eighteenth-century

artists reworked sixteenth-century paintings; rebranding Elizabeth in their own style. For example, one heavily overpainted portrait of the Queen (fig. 101), which bears a striking similarity to the frontispiece to Heywood's play, obscures a far more elaborate original costume and veil, similar to that seen in the Ditchley portrait and the woodcut from the 1590s. Remarkably, the Queen's features have also been enhanced to those of an early-eighteenth-century beauty, in order to perpetuate her reputation at this later date.

Fig. 100 (right) Title page to *If you know not me, You know no bodie: Or, The troubles of Queene Elizabeth*, by Thomas Heywood, 1605 edition (British Library)

Fig. 101 (opposite) Elizabeth I, unknown artist, early seventeenth century with eighteenth-century overpainting (National Portrait Gallery, London)

SELECT BIBLIOGRAPHY

J. Arnold, 'The "Coronation" Portrait of Elizabeth I', *The Burlington Magazine,* 120, no. 908, 1978, pp.726–39, 741

A. Belsey and C. Belsey, 'Icons of Divinity: Portraits of Elizabeth I', L. Gent and N. Llewellyn (eds), *Renaissance Bodies: The Human Figure in English Culture* c.1540–1660 (Reaktion Books, London, 1990), pp.11–35

P. Collinson, 'Elizabeth I', *Oxford Dictionary of National Biography* (Oxford University Press, 2004), XVIII, pp.95–130

A. Connolly and L. Hopkins (eds), *Goddesses and Queens: The Iconography of Elizabeth I* (Manchester University Press, 2007)

T. Cooper, 'The Queen's Visual Presence', S. Doran (ed.), *Elizabeth: The Exhibition at the National Maritime Museum* (Chatto & Windus in association with the National Maritime Museum, London, 2003), pp.175–81

T. Cooper, *A Guide to Tudor & Jacobean Portraits* (National Portrait Gallery Publications, London, 2008)

T. Cooper with J. Eade, *Elizabeth I & her People* (National Portrait Gallery, London, 2013)

S. Doran, 'Virginity, Divinity and Power: The Portraits of Elizabeth I' in S. Doran and T.S. Freeman (eds), *The Myth of Elizabeth I* (Palgrave Macmillan, Basingstoke, 2003), pp.171–99

S. Frye, *Elizabeth I: The Competition for Representation* (OUP, New York, 1993)

K. Hearn (ed.), *Dynasties: Painting in Tudor and Jacobean England, 1530–1630* (Tate Publishing, London, 1995), pp.78–90, 122

J.R. Jewitt, '"Eliza Fortuna": Reconsidering the Ditchley Portrait of Elizabeth I', *The Burlington Magazine*, 156, no.1334, 2014, pp.293–8

O. Millar, *Tudor, Stuart and Early Georgian Pictures in the Royal Collection*, 2 vols (Phaidon Press, London, 1963), I, p.65

R. Strong, *Portraits of Queen Elizabeth I* (Clarendon Press, Oxford, 1963)

— 'Elizabeth I', *Tudor and Jacobean Portraits,* National Portrait Gallery, *2 vols* (HMSO, London, 1969), I, pp.99–112

— *The Cult of Elizabeth: Elizabethan Portraiture and Pageantry* (University of California Press, Berkeley and Los Angeles, 1977)

— *Gloriana: The Portraits of Queen Elizabeth I* (Thames & Hudson, London, 1987)

NOTES

1 R. Brown (ed.), *Calendar of state papers and manuscripts, relating to English affairs, existing in the archives and collections of Venice* (*CSPV*), 38 vols (Longman, Green, Longman, Roberts and Green, London, 1864–1947), VI, pt 2, p.1058. For discussion of this quote, see Strong 1963, p.18.

2 W.B. Rye (ed.), *England as seen by Foreigners in the Days of Elizabeth and James I* (J.T. Smith, London, 1865). See also Strong 1963, pp.18–19.

3 E.H. Fellowes (ed.), *English Madrigal Verse, 1585–1632* (Clarendon Press, Oxford, 1920), p.432

4 Strong, 1963, p.25

5 J. Evelyn, *Sculptura*, C.F. Bell (ed.), (Clarendon Press, Oxford, 1906), p.25

6 L.S. Marcus, J. Mueller and M.B. Rose (eds), *Elizabeth I: Collected Works* (University of Chicago Press, Chicago, 2000), p.35

7 *CSPV*, VI, pt 2, p.1058

8 J.A. Lawson (ed.), *The Elizabethan New Year's Gift Exchanges 1559–1603*, Records of Social and Economic History, new series 51 (published for the British Academy by Oxford University Press, 2013), p.41 (59.149); p.61 (62.147)

9 'Book Review', *Archaeologia, or Miscellaneous Tracts Relating to Antiquity* (1770–1992, Jan. 1773), British Periodicals, vol. 2, pp.169–70

10 J. Fletcher, 'The date of the portrait of Elizabeth I in her Coronation Robes', *The Burlington Magazine,*

120: no.908, 1978, pp.726 and 753. Ian Tyers undertook further dendrochronological analysis in 2009, which revised the date of the last heartwood tree rings from 1572, 1574 and 1577 to 1576, 1577 and 1581 as a result of cross-referencing with data from Eastern Baltic oak.

11 N. Hilliard, *A Treatise Concerning The Arte of Limning*, R.K.R. Thornton & T.G.S. Cain (eds) (Carcanet, Ashington, 1992), p.67

12 In 1584, Hilliard gave Elizabeth a New Year's gift described as a 'faire Table being pyctures Conteyninge the history of the five wise virgins and the five follysshe virgins'. See Lawson, op. cit., p.330 (84.190).

13 For example, the Earl of Ormonde gave the Queen a phoenix jewel made of gold rubies and diamonds in 1578. See Lawson, op. cit., p.226 (78.21).

14 K. van Mander, *The Lives of the Illustrious Netherlandish and German Painters, from the first edition of the Schilder-boeck 1604*, Hessel Miedema (ed.), 6 vols (Doornspijk, 1994–6), V, p.126

15 Strong, 1963, p.7

16 Marcus etc, op. cit.

ELIZABETH I REVEALED

Elizabeth I
Unknown Continental artist, *c.*1575
Oil on panel, 1130×787mm
NPG 2082

The underdrawing revealed in this image using infrared reflectography shows how the artist kept quite closely to the drawn design but made lots of sketchy marks to capture the Queen's left hand. The feathered fan was also originally designed to be slightly higher, as seen from the altered position.

Photography in ultraviolet light shows up the areas of recent restoration as dark marks. Small areas of old damage in the face and hands can be seen, but, given the age of the picture, most of the paint remains in very good condition. The thin strip of panel to the far left is a later addition and must have been replaced following early damage to the picture.

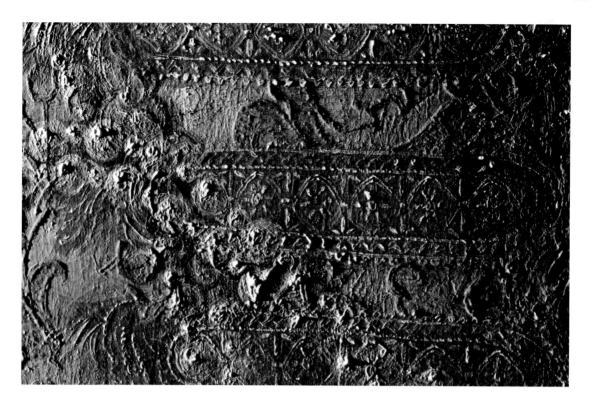

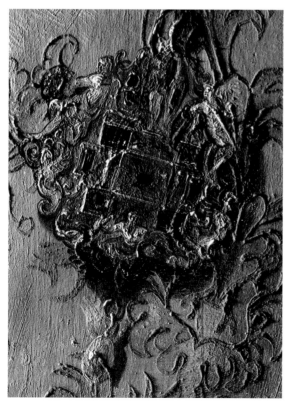

Details of the clothing and jewels taken in raking light demonstrate how the artist used a thick paint to create texture in these areas, helping to develop a greater sense of three-dimensionality.

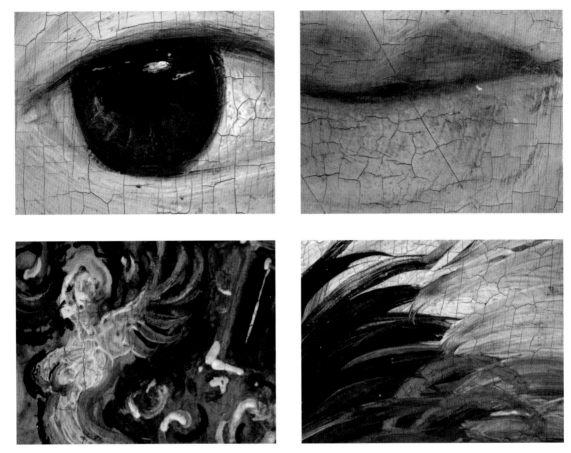

These details highlight the skill and confidence of the artist, who in some places was swiftly blending wet paint together, as in the detail of the fan (above, bottom right), to create a sense of movement.

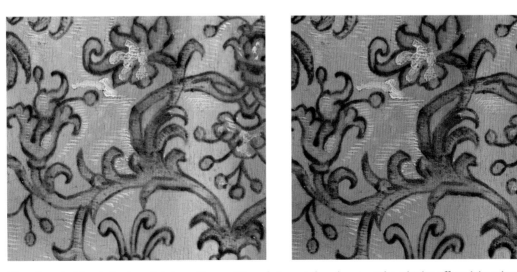

The colours in this painting have faded over time, and the red pigments have become paler. This has affected the colouring of the Queen's dress, which would originally have been much stronger, as suggested in the digital reconstruction shown here.

As one of the few surviving portraits of Elizabeth painted from the life, this image of the Queen's face in her early forties is an important record of her appearance at the height of her reign. Although her face looks very pale today, analysis has shown that a red pigment (known as red lake), used in her face, has faded. This evidence indicates that she would originally have had rosier cheeks; at this point in her life Elizabeth may have had a natural complexion and probably did not wear pale make-up.

The wooden panel is made from oak derived from a tree felled in the Baltic region after 1561.
Wood from this region was regularly imported into England at this date, and the majority of wood
used for panel paintings in this period derives from this area. The diamond-shaped blocks on the
back were added at a later date to strengthen the joints and the structure of the panel.

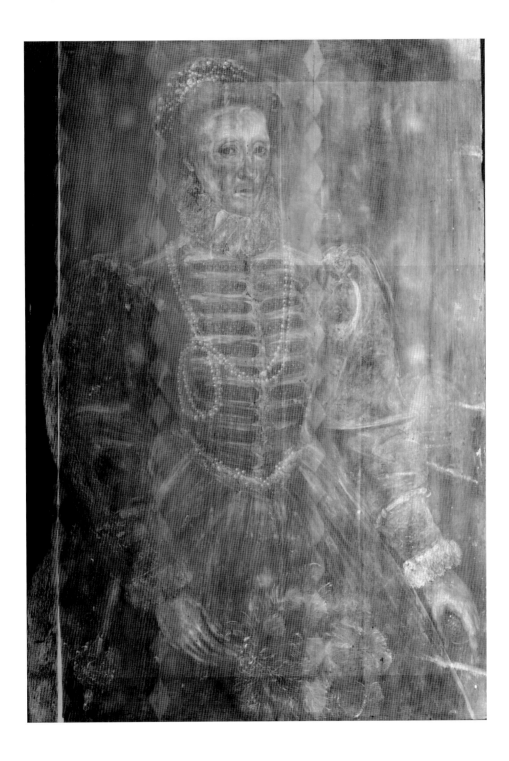

X-radiography shows some adjustments to Elizabeth's right hand. Such images can often
be difficult to read because they show the structure of the panel as well as the paint layers.

GLOSSARY

Abrasion Damage caused to upper paint layers, usually as a result of rubbing or scraping.

Azurite A bright blue copper carbonate mineral, used as a pigment.

Bodycolour Watercolour that is mixed with white pigment to make it opaque. It is often used in drawings on tinted paper or watercolours to show the contrast with the transparency of pure watercolour.

Brushwork The characteristics of the paint surface in relation to the application of paint using a brush.

Canvas Woven stretched cloth, usually made from linen but sometimes from cotton. Oil paintings themselves are often called canvases.

Cartellino A small piece of paper or parchment that is painted illusionistically within the composition of a painting.

Cartoon This term originally referred to the full-scale preliminary sketch made for a painting. This outline, usually done in chalk or charcoal, was then transferred on to the painting support.

Chalk A drawing material, similar in texture and appearance to pastel, made from various soft stones or earths.

Craquelure A pattern of cracks in the paint caused by flexing within the support over time.

Cross-section A slice through a minute sample of paint that shows the layer structure. It is used to identify pigments.

Dendrochronology An examination of the sequence of tree rings in the end grain of a wood panel, which can help to provide the earliest possible felling dates for the wood used for the panel. The technique can also indicate the geographical origin of the wood.

Dowel A small wooden peg employed to align two boards during panel construction. A hole is bored into the edge of the boards and the dowel inserted.

Earth pigments A group of pigments – including ochres, siennas and umbers – made from naturally occurring coloured deposits containing iron oxide. They are usually browns, reds, yellows and oranges.

Engaged frame A frame attached to a panel when it was made, and prepared with the panel before painting.

Gilding The application of a thin layer of gold or gold leaf to a surface using an adhesive binder.

Glaze A transparent layer of paint brushed over a dried underlayer. Generally associated with oil painting, glazes can also be applied on top of each other to create the appearance of depth and luminosity.

Ground The layer used to prepare a support for painting and upon which to apply the paint.

Impasto Thick paint that has been applied with a brush, knife or fingers resulting in a variety of textures on the surface of the painting.

Infrared reflectography (IRR) Infrared light has a longer wavelength than visible light and can penetrate the upper paint layers but is absorbed by others beneath, particularly underdrawing containing carbon.

Lake pigments Pigments manufactured by precipitating dyes made from natural sources on to inert binders. Lakes can be red, yellow, and red- or yellow-brown. They generally form translucent paint when mixed with oil, and are prone to fading when exposed to light.

Lead soap Lead soap aggregates can form through interaction between the oil medium and lead pigments, and push up through the paint layers, forming lumps or 'protrusions' at the surface of the painting.

Lead-tin yellow A bright yellow pigment manufactured from a compound of lead and tin. Not generally used after about 1750.

Lead white A white pigment composed of basic lead carbonate. It was the only white pigment available until the late eighteenth century.

Medium The substance that carries the pigment to form paint. The term can also be used more generally to refer to the materials of the work.

Mordant gilding Laying gold leaf on to a pigmented oil layer that has been applied to define the elements that are to be gilded. The gold is applied when the mordant is still tacky.

Oil paint Pigment mixed with an oil medium, usually linseed. It dries slowly, rather than sets, and can be painted over to create a great variety of effects. Both minute detail and subtle blending of tones can be achieved.

Overpainting Application of non-original paint that wholly or partially covers the original.

Paint sampling A method of identifying pigments. Analysis can help with dating and reveal the order of the paint layers.

Panel A solid painting support, made from a single board of wood, or two or more joined together.

Pattern A preliminary drawing made to be used to transfer the image to a prepared support before painting.

Pentimento The traditional art-historical term for an alteration made by the artist to the composition during the painting process (plural *pentimenti*).

Photomicrograph A close-up image taken through a microscope at a high magnification.

Pigment Small particles of solid substances that form the coloured component of paint, carried by the medium to form paint. Different pigments deteriorate at different rates over time.

Pouncing A method of transferring a preparatory drawing for a painting on to another surface. Holes are pricked around the outlines of a drawing and then powdered chalk or charcoal is dusted through the holes, producing a dotted outline of the design on the surface of the support.

Priming A layer of paint applied over the ground (and sometimes over the underdrawing) to provide a coloured toning or preparation layer for the paint.

Provenance The history of a painting's ownership.

Raking light The illumination of the painting from only one side at an oblique angle to the surface. It is used to reveal the surface texture of a painting.

Retouching The work done by a restorer to replace areas of loss or damage in a painting.

Smalt A blue pigment made from ground cobalt blue glass. In an oil medium it has a tendency to discolour.

Support The surface on which a painting or drawing is executed.

Surface examination An examination of the construction of paint layers, glazes and condition, often made using a microscope. This method provides important evidence concerning an artist's technique and paint handling.

Ultraviolet examination Ultraviolet light has a shorter wavelength than visible light. When exposed to ultraviolet light, some materials fluoresce (give off visible light). Aged resin-based varnishes fluoresce green while restoration applied on top of old varnishes appears black.

Underdrawing The preliminary drawing, or marking out of the pattern of the composition, drawn freehand or traced on to the ground, before the application of priming or paint layers.

Wet-in-wet The process of laying down one colour on top of or beside another colour before the first layer is dry, which allows for some intermingling of the colours.

X-radiography The exposure of photographic film to short electromagnetic waves passed through a painting to create an image, which can show alterations to the composition that may otherwise have remained hidden. Pigments containing heavy metals show up as white.

PICTURE CREDITS

The National Portrait Gallery would like to thank the copyright holders for granting permission to reproduce works illustrated in this book. Every effort has been made to contact the holders of the copyright materials, and any omissions will be corrected in future editions if the publisher is notified in writing.

Dimensions for figures are given height × width (mm), where available.

Figures marked with an asterisk denote works in the *Real Tudors* display at the National Portrait Gallery, London, (12 September 2014–1 March 2015).

Fig. 1 *The Family of Henry VII with St. George and the Dragon*, by an unknown Flemish artist, c.1503–9. Oil on panel, 1456 × 1426mm. Photo: Royal Collection Trust/© Her Majesty Queen Elizabeth II 2014.

Fig. 2 Henry VII, by an unknown English artist, early sixteenth century. Oil on panel, 380 × 245mm. Photo: Society of Antiquaries of London/Bridgeman Art Library.

Fig. 3 Elizabeth of York, by an unknown English artist, early sixteenth century. Oil on panel, 387 × 278mm. Photo: Royal Collection Trust/© Her Majesty Queen Elizabeth II 2014.

*Fig. 4 (see also pp.10–11 and 30) Henry VII, by an unknown Netherlandish artist, 1505. Oil on panel, 425 × 305mm. Photo: © National Portrait Gallery, London (NPG 416). Purchased, 1876.

Fig. 5 Margaret of Austria, attributed to Pieter van Coninxloo, c.1500. Oil on panel, 367 × 225mm. Photo: Royal Collection Trust/© Her Majesty Queen Elizabeth II 2014.

*Fig. 6 Funeral effigy of Henry VII, attributed to Pietro Torrigiano, 1509. Painted plaster and wood. Photo: © Dean and Chapter of Westminster.

Fig. 7 Funeral effigy of Elizabeth of York, by Lawrence Emler, 1503. Photo: © Dean and Chapter of Westminster.

Fig. 8 Henry VII portrait bust by Pietro Torrigiano, 1509–11. Painted terracotta. Height: 606mm; width: 690mm; depth: 360mm. Photo: © V&A Images.

Fig. 9 Detail of Henry VII and Elizabeth of York's tomb in the Lady Chapel, Westminster Abbey. Pietro Torrigiano, 1512–17, gilt bronze. Photo: © Dean and Chapter of Westminster.

Fig. 10 Henry VII, by John Payne, 1622. Line engraving, 157 × 109mm (paper size). Photo: © National Portrait Gallery, London (D23824). Given by the daughter of compiler William Fleming MD, Mary Elizabeth Stopford, 1931.

Fig. 11 Cartoon for the *Whitehall Mural*, showing Henry VIII and Henry VII, by Hans Holbein the Younger, 1536–7. Drawing, ink and watercolour on paper, 2578 × 1372mm. Photo: © National Portrait Gallery, London (NPG 4027). Accepted in lieu of tax by H.M. Government and allocated to the Gallery, 1957.

Fig. 12 Detail from *Henry VII, Elizabeth of York, Henry VIII and Jane Seymour*, by Remigius van Leemput, 1667. Oil on canvas, 889 × 992mm. Photo: Royal Collection Trust/© Her Majesty Queen Elizabeth II 2014.

*Fig. 13 Henry VII, by an unknown artist, late sixteenth century. Oil on panel, 572 × 445mm. Photo: © National Portrait Gallery, London (NPG 4980(13)). Purchased, 1974.

Fig. 14 Digital infrared reflectogram detail of Fig. 13. Photo: courtesy Tager Stonor Richardson; © National Portrait Gallery, London.

HENRY VIII

Fig. 15 Foot combat armour of King Henry VIII, English, 1520. Steel. Height: 1880m. Photo: © Royal Armouries.

Fig. 16 Field armour of Henry VIII, Italian, c.1544. Steel, blackened, etched, and gilt; textile; leather. Height: 1840mm. Photo: Metropolitan Museum of Art, New York, Photo: Scala.

*Fig. 17 (see also pp.36–7 and 58) Henry VIII, by an unknown Anglo–Netherlandish artist, c.1520. Oil on panel, 508 × 381mm. Photo: © National Portrait Gallery, London (NPG 4690). Purchased, 1969.

Fig. 18 Katherine of Aragon, by an unknown Anglo–Netherlandish artist, c.1520s. Oil on oak panel, 520 × 420mm. Photo: © National Portrait Gallery, London (L246). Lent by Church Commissioners for England, 2011.

Fig. 19 Henry VIII, by Lucas Horenbout, 1526–7. Watercolour on vellum laid on playing card, 47mm diameter. Photo: Royal Collection Trust/© Her Majesty Queen Elizabeth II 2014.

*Fig. 20 Henry VIII, by Joos van Cleve, c.1530–5. Oil on panel, 724 × 586mm, RCIN403368. The Royal Collection RCIN/HM The Queen. Photo: Royal Collection Trust/© Her Majesty Queen Elizabeth II 2014.

Fig. 21 François I, after Joos van Cleve, c.1530. Oil on panel, 375 × 317mm. Photo: Royal Collection Trust/© Her Majesty Queen Elizabeth II 2014.

*Fig. 22 Henry VIII, by an unknown Anglo–Netherlandish artist, 1535–40. Oil on panel, 584 × 445mm. Photo: © National Portrait Gallery, London (NPG 3638). Given by Sir Geoffrey Langdon Keynes, 1948.

*Fig. 23 Henry VIII, by an unknown Anglo–Netherlandish artist, 1535–40. Oil on panel, 572 × 425mm. Photo: © National Portrait Gallery, London (NPG 1376). Purchased, 1904.

Fig. 24 Henry VIII, by an unknown Anglo–Netherlandish artist, c.1540. Oil on panel, 545 × 380mm panel. Photo: Art Gallery of New South Wales.

Fig. 25 Henry VIII, by an unknown Anglo–Netherlandish artist, 1535–40. Oil on panel, 480 × 345mm. Photo: Society of Antiquaries of London/Bridgeman Art Library.

Fig. 26 Photomicrograph of fig. 23. Photo: © National Portrait Gallery, London.

Fig. 27 Photomicrograph of fig. 23. Photo: © National Portrait Gallery, London.

Fig. 28 Christina of Denmark, by Hans Holbein the Younger, 1538. Oil on panel, 1791 × 826mm. Photo: National Gallery, London, Photo Scala.

Fig. 29 Henry VIII, by Hans Holbein the Younger, c.1536–7. Oil on panel, 280 × 200mm. Photo: Thyssen-Bornemisza Collection, Madrid, Photo Scala.

Fig. 30 Detail of the figure of Henry VIII from the *Whitehall Mural* cartoon, by Hans Holbein the Younger, 1536–7. Ink and watercolour, 2578 × 1372mm. Photo: © National Portrait Gallery, London. Accepted in lieu of tax by H.M. Government and allocated to the Gallery, 1957.

Fig. 31 Detail of fig. 30. Photo: © National Portrait Gallery, London.

Fig. 32 *Henry VII, Elizabeth of York, Henry VIII and Jane Seymour*, by Remigius van Leemput, 1667. Oil on canvas, 889 × 992mm. Photo: Royal Collection Trust/© Her Majesty Queen Elizabeth II 2014.

*Fig. 33 Henry VIII, by an unknown artist, 1540s. Oil on panel, 2375 × 1207mm. Petworth House, the Egremont Collection. Photo: © National Trust Images/Derrick E. Witty.

Fig. 34 Title page to *When You See me, You Know Me. Or the famous Chronicle Historie of king Henrie the Eight, with the birth and vertuous life of Edward Prince of Wales, etc.* by Samuel Rowley, 1613. Photo: © The British Library Board.

*Fig. 35 Henry VIII, by an unknown artist, late sixteenth century. Oil on panel, 582 × 450mm. Photo: © National Portrait Gallery, London (NPG 4980(14)). Purchased, 1974.

EDWARD VI

Fig. 36 Edward VI, by Hans Holbein the Younger, probably 1538. Oil on panel, 568 × 440mm. Photo: National Gallery of Art, Washington, Andrew W. Mellon Collection 1937.1.64.

*Fig. 37 Edward VI's 'Chronicle', 1537–53. Bound manuscript on paper with tooled leather binding. Photo shows page from 1547, British Library Cotton Ms Nero C.x, f.12. Photo: © The British Library Board. The British Library, London.

Fig. 38 Edward VI, by Hans Holbein the Younger, *c.*1540–2. Black and coloured chalks and pen and ink on pale pink prepared paper, 273 × 227mm. Photo: Royal Collection Trust/© Her Majesty Queen Elizabeth II 2014.

*Fig. 39 Edward VI, after Hans Holbein the Younger, *c.*1542. Oil on panel, 438 × 311mm. Photo: © National Portrait Gallery, London (NPG 1132). Purchased, 1898.

*Figs 40 and 41 Edward VI, attributed to Guillim Scrots, 1546. Oil on panel, 425 × 1600mm. Photos: © National Portrait Gallery, London (NPG 1299). Purchased, 1901.

Fig. 42 X-ray detail of figs 40 and 41. Photo: © National Portrait Gallery, London.

*Fig. 43 Edward VI, by an unknown artist after Guillim Scrots, *c.*1546. Oil on panel, 473 × 279mm. Photo: © National Portrait Gallery, London (NPG 442). Purchased, 1877.

Figs 44 and 45 Details of figs 40 and 41. Photos: © National Portrait Gallery, London.

*Fig. 46 (see also pp.64–5 and 88) Edward VI, associated with the workshop of 'Master John', *c.*1547. Oil on panel, 1556 × 813mm. Photo: © National Portrait Gallery, London (NPG 5511). Purchased, 1982.

Fig. 47 Edward VI, attributed to Guillim Scrots, *c.*1546. Oil on panel, 1072 × 820mm. Photo: Royal Collection Trust/© Her Majesty Queen Elizabeth II 2014.

*Fig. 48 Edward VI, by an unknown Anglo–Netherlandish workshop, 1547. Oil on canvas, 1715 × 1070mm. Lord Egremont Collection. Photo: © Lord Egremont Collection.

Fig. 49 Edward VI, attributed to Guillim Scrots, *c.*1550. Oil on canvas, 1680 × 870mm. Photo: © RMN-Grand Palais (Musée du Louvre)/ Thierry Ollivier.

Fig. 50 Elizabeth of Valois, by François Clouet, *c.*1549. Watercolour on vellum, 34mm diameter. Photo: Royal Collection Trust/ © Her Majesty Queen Elizabeth II 2014.

Fig. 51 Title page to William Tyndale's translation of the New Testament, London, 1552. Photo: Rare Bible collection, Museum of Biblical Art, New York.

Fig. 52 *A description of Master Latimer, preaching before King Edward the sixth, in the preaching place at Westminster*, by an unknown artist, late sixteenth century. Woodcut, paper size 145 × 181mm. Photo: © National Portrait Gallery, London (NPG D23050). Purchased, 1966.

*Fig. 53 Edward VI and the Pope, by an unknown artist, *c.*1575. Oil on panel, 622 × 908mm. Photo: © National Portrait Gallery, London (NPG 4165). Purchased, 1960.

Fig. 54 Detail of fig. 53. Photo: © National Portrait Gallery, London.

LADY JANE GREY

Fig. 55 Edward VI's 'devise for the succession', written in his own hand, 1553. Photo: Inner Temple Library.

Fig. 56 (see also pp.94–5) Lady Jane Dudley (née Grey), by an unknown artist, *c.*1590–1600. Oil on panel, 856 × 603mm. Photo: © National Portrait Gallery, London (NPG 6804). Purchased with help from the proceeds of the 150th anniversary gala, 2006.

Fig. 57 Lady Jane Dudley (née Grey), by Magdalena de Passe, Willem de Passe, published by Frans van den Wyngaerde (Wijngaerde), 1620. Line engraving, 164 × 115mm plate size; 179 × 130mm paper size. © National Portrait Gallery, London (NPG D21393).

MARY I

*Fig. 58 Mary I, attributed to Lucas Horenbout (or Hornebolte), *c.*1525. Watercolour on vellum, 35mm sight diameter. © National Portrait Gallery, London (NPG 6453). Purchased, 1999.

Fig. 59 Photomicrograph detail of fig. 58. Photo: © National Portrait Gallery, London.

*Fig. 60 Mary I, by Master John, 1544. Oil on panel, 711 × 508mm. Photo: © National Portrait Gallery, London (NPG 428). Purchased, 1876.

Fig. 61 Katherine Parr, attributed to Master John, *c.*1545. Oil on panel, 1803 × 940mm. Photo: © National Portrait Gallery, London (NPG 4451). Purchased with help from the Gulbenkian Foundation, 1965.

Figs 62 and 63 Photomicrograph details of figs 60 and 61. Photo: © National Portrait Gallery, London.

*Fig. 64 *The Queen Mary Book of Prayers*, unknown artist, *c.*1554. Illuminated manuscript on vellum, 205 × 310mm (double-page open folio). By kind permission of the Administrator of Westminster Cathedral. Photo: © Westminster Cathedral; photographer: David Lambert.

*Fig. 65 Mary I, Hans Eworth, 1544. Oil on panel, 1040 × 785mm. Loaned by kind permission of the Society of Antiquaries, London. Photo: © Society of Antiquaries of London.

Fig. 66 Philip II, by an unknown artist after Titian, late sixteenth century. Oil on panel, 639 × 476mm. Photo: Royal Collection Trust/© Her Majesty Queen Elizabeth II 2014.

*Fig. 67 (see also pp.102–3 and 122) Mary I, by Hans Eworth, 1554. Oil on panel, 216 × 169mm. © National Portrait Gallery, London (NPG 4861). Purchased with help from The Art Fund, the Pilgrim Trust, H.M. Government, Miss Elizabeth Taylor and Richard Burton, 1972.

Fig. 68 Mary I, by Anthonis Mor, 1554. Oil on panel, 1090 × 840mm. Photo: Museo del Prado, Madrid.

*Fig. 69 Philip II, by an unknown artist after Titian, 1555. Oil on panel, 86 × 64mm. Photo: © National Portrait Gallery, London (NPG 4175). Given by Edward Peter Jones, 1960.

*Fig. 70 Mary I, by an unknown artist after Anthonis Mor, 1555. Oil on panel, 86 × 64mm. Photo: © National Portrait Gallery, London (NPG 4174). Given by Edward Peter Jones, 1960.

Fig. 71 *Henry VIII enthroned under a canopy on a dais, flanked on each side by his successors; Mary and Philip on the left with Mars behind them, and Elizabeth on the right*, after Lucas de Heere, *c.*1595–1600. Engraving on paper, 360 × 491mm. Photo: © The Trustees of the British Museum.

*Fig. 72 Mary I, by an unknown artist, late sixteenth century. Oil on panel, 572 × 451mm. Photo: © National Portrait Gallery, London (NPG 4980(16)). Purchased, 1974.

ELIZABETH I

Figs 73, 74 and 75 *Henry VIII and Family*, by an unknown artist, sixteenth century, *c*.1545. Oil on canvas, 1445 × 3559mm. Photo: Royal Collection Trust/© Her Majesty Queen Elizabeth II 2014.

Fig. 76 *Elizabeth I and the Three Goddesses*, by Hans Eworth, 1569. Oil on panel, 629 × 844mm. Photo: Royal Collection Trust/ © Her Majesty Queen Elizabeth II 2014.

*Fig. 77 *Elizabeth I and the Three Goddesses*, attributed to Isaac Oliver, *c*.1590. Watercolour and bodycolour, heightened with gold, on vellum stuck to card, 115 × 157mm. © National Portrait Gallery, London (NPG 6947). Purchased, 2012.

Fig. 78 Elizabeth I, attributed to Guillim Scrots, *c*.1546. Oil on panel, 1085 × 818mm. Photo: Royal Collection Trust/© Her Majesty Queen Elizabeth II 2014.

*Fig. 79 Elizabeth I, by an unknown English artist, *c*.1560. Oil on panel, 394 × 273mm. Photo: © National Portrait Gallery, London (NPG 4449). Purchased, 1965.

Figs 80 and 81 Detail of fig. 79. Photo: © National Portrait Gallery, London.

*Fig. 82 Elizabeth I, by an unknown English artist, late sixteenth century. Gouache on vellum laid on card, 89 × 56mm. Photo: Private Collection.

*Fig. 83 Elizabeth I, by an unknown English artist, *c*.1600. Oil on panel, 1273 × 997mm. Photo: © National Portrait Gallery, London (NPG 5175). Purchased, 1978.

*Fig. 84 Elizabeth I, by Nicholas Hilliard, 1572. Watercolour on vellum, 51 × 48mm (oval). Photo: © National Portrait Gallery, London (NPG 108). Purchased, 1860.

Figs 85 and 86 Photomicrograph details of fig. 84. Photos: © National Portrait Gallery, London.

Fig. 87 Elizabeth I, associated with Nicholas Hilliard, *c*.1575, with detail showing Pelican jewel. Oil on panel, 788 × 613mm, Walker Art Gallery, Liverpool. Photo: Courtesy National Museums Liverpool.

*Fig. 88 Elizabeth I, associated with Nicholas Hilliard, *c*.1575, with detail showing Phoenix jewel. Oil on panel, 787 × 610mm. Photo: © National Portrait Gallery, London (NPG 190). Purchased, 1865.

Fig. 89 Detail of fig. 88 using infrared reflectography. Photo: courtesy Tager Stonor Richardson, © National Portrait Gallery, London.

*Fig. 90 (see also pp.2, 126–7 and 162) Elizabeth I, by an unknown continental artist, *c*.1575. Oil on panel, 1130 × 787mm. Photo: © National Portrait Gallery, London (NPG 2082). Purchased, 1925.

Fig. 91 Elizabeth I, by Frederico Zuccaro, 1575. Black and red chalk on paper, 307 × 222mm. Photo: © The Trustees of the British Museum.

Fig. 92 Elizabeth I, by Marcus Gheeraerts the Elder, *c*.1585. Oil on panel, 457 × 381 mm. Photo: Private Collection.

Fig. 93 Elizabeth I, by an unknown artist, *c*.1585–90. Oil on panel, 953 × 819mm. Photo: © National Portrait Gallery, London (NPG 2471). Given by wish of Sir Aston Webb, 1930.

Fig. 94 Elizabeth I, by an unknown English artist, *c*.1588. Oil on panel, 1330 × 1050mm. Photo: reproduced by kind permission of His Grace the Duke of Bedford and the Trustees of the Bedford Estates.

*Fig. 95 Elizabeth I, by an unknown English artist, *c*.1588. Oil on panel, 1105 × 1270mm. Tyrwhitt-Drake Collection. Photo: © Tyrwhitt-Drake Collection.

*Fig. 96 Elizabeth I, by an unknown English artist, *c*.1588. Oil on panel, 978 × 724mm. Photo: © National Portrait Gallery, London (NPG 541). Transferred from British Museum, 1879.

Fig. 97 Elizabeth I, by Isaac Oliver, 1590–2. Watercolour on vellum stuck to a playing card, 82 × 52mm. Photo: © V&A Images.

Fig. 98 *Elizabetha Regina*, by an unknown artist, late sixteenth century. Woodcut, 500 × 369mm. Photo: © Ashmolean Museum, University of Oxford.

*Fig. 99 Elizabeth I, by Marcus Gheeraerts the Younger, *c*.1592. Oil on canvas, 2413 × 1524mm. Photo: © National Portrait Gallery, London (NPG 2561). Bequeathed by Harold Lee-Dillon, Seventeenth Viscount Dillon, 1932.

Fig. 100 Title page to *If you know not me, you know no bodie: or, The troubles of Queene Elizabeth*, Thomas Heywood, 1605 edition. Photo: The Huntington Library.

*Fig. 101 Elizabeth I, unknown artist, early seventeenth century with eighteenth-century overpainting. Oil on panel, 851 × 670mm. Photo: © National Portrait Gallery, London (NPG 542). Transferred from British Museum, 1879.

TIMELINES

pp.12–13

Henry VII. See fig. 4.

Pembroke Castle. Photo: Laura Kudelska/Alamy.

Elizabeth of York (see fig. 3). Unknown English artist, early sixteenth century. Oil on panel, 387 × 278mm. Photo: Royal Collection Trust/© Her Majesty Queen Elizabeth II 2014.

Henry VI. Unknown English artist, *c*.1540. Oil on panel, 318 × 254mm. Photo: © National Portrait Gallery, London. (NPG 2457). Purchased, 1930.

Edward IV. Unknown English artist, *c*. 1540. Oil on panel, 1330 × 273 mm. Photo: © National Portrait Gallery, London (NPG 3542). Purchased, 1947.

Richard III. Unknown artist, late sixteenth century (late fifteenth century). Oil on panel, 638 × 470mm. Photo: © National Portrait Gallery, London (NPG 148). Given by James Thomson Gibson-Craig, 1862.

Margaret Beaufort. Unknown artist, second half of sixteenth century. Oil on panel, 686 × 549mm. Photo: © National Portrait Gallery, London (NPG 551). Transferred from British Museum, 1879.

Katherine of Aragon. See Fig. 18.

Prince Arthur. Unknown English artist, sixteenth century. Oil on panel, 388 × 279mm. Photo: Royal Collection Trust/ © Her Majesty Queen Elizabeth II 2014.

pp.38–9

Henry VIII. See fig. 17.

Prince Arthur. See credit line for pp.12–13 above.

Katherine of Aragon. See credit line for pp. 12–13 above.

Cardinal Wolsey. Unknown artist, late sixteenth century (*c*.1520). Oil on panel, 838 × 559mm. Photo: © National Portrait Gallery, London (NPG 32). Purchased, 1858.

Anne Boleyn. Unknown artist, late sixteenth century (*c*.1533–6). Oil on panel, 543 × 416mm. Photo: © National Portrait Gallery, London (NPG 668). Purchased, 1882.

Thomas More. After Hans Holbein the Younger, early seventeenth century (1527). Oil on panel, 749 × 584mm. Photo: © National Portrait Gallery, London (NPG 4358). Purchased with help from the Pilgrim Trust, Stanley Morison, Kenneth More and the Sir Thomas More Appeal Fund, 1964.

Thomas Cromwell. After Hans Holbein the Younger, early seventeenth century (1533–4). Oil on panel, 781 × 619mm. Photo: © National Portrait Gallery, London (NPG 1727). Purchased, 1914.

St George's Chapel, Windsor. Photo: Peter Phipp/Travelshots.com/ Alamy.

Katherine Parr. See fig. 61.

Ruins of Fountains Abbey. Photo: © National Trust Images/ Sylvaine Poitau.

INDEX